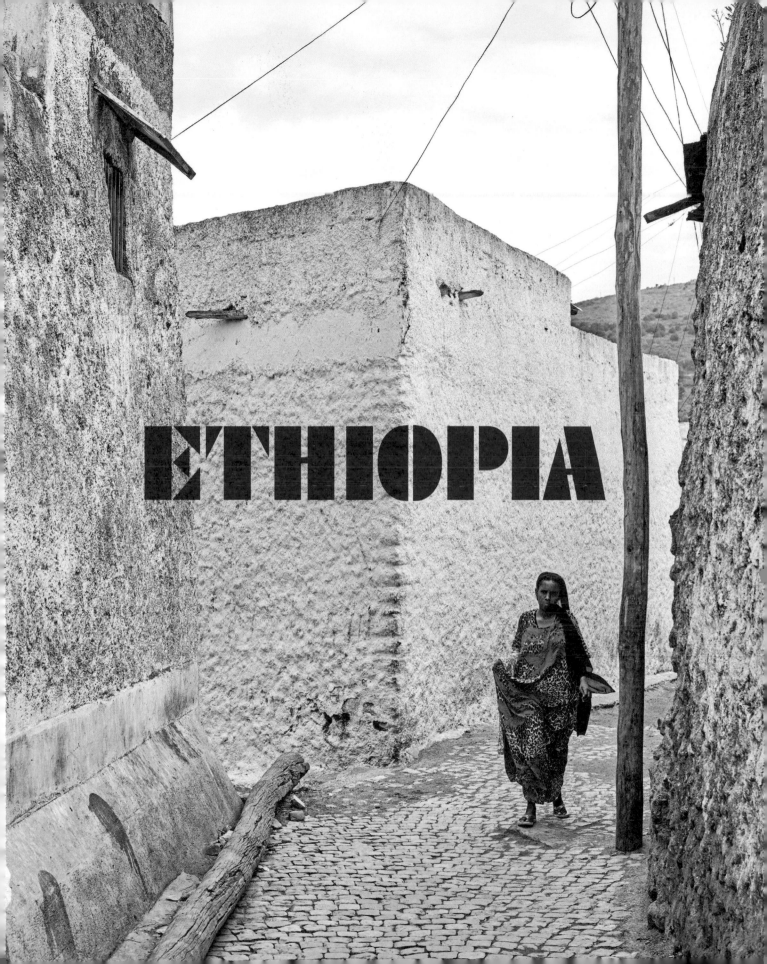

ETHIOPIA

RECIPES AND TRADITIONS FROM THE HORN OF AFRICA

YOHANIS GEBREYESUS With Jeff Koehler

For my mother, Senait, who has shown me, more than she knows, how to understand food through olfaction; and to the Paul Bocuse Institute team, who taught me about "the magic of service when it is included."

First published in 2019 by
INTERLINK BOOKS
An imprint of Interlink Publishing Group, Inc.
46 Crosby Street, Northampton, MA 01060
www.interlinkbooks.com

Library of Congress Cataloging-in-Publication Data available
ISBN 978-1-62371-963-0

Co-author: Jeff Koehler
Editors: Judith Hannam and Hannah Coughlin
American Edition Editor: Leyla Moushabeck
Photography: Peter Cassidy
Food Stylist: Linda Tubby
Props Stylist: Wei Tang
Designer: Paul Palmer-Edwards, GradeDesign.com
Map design: Yohanis Gebreyesus
Production: Gemma John and Nic Jones

Printed in China

10 9 8 7 6 5 4 3 2 1

Contents

Introduction 6

1 Injera & Flatbreads 14

2 Seasonings 36

3 Breakfast 56

4 Vegetables & Fresh Cheese 74

5 Legumes & Grains 100

6 Beef, Lamb & Goat 124

7 Poultry, Eggs & Fish 168

8 Snacks & Drinks 196

Index 220

Acknowledgments 224

Introduction:
Cuisine from the Land of Origins

ዘርዓያዕቆብ (በላዩ ሑአንየለ ዘመሳ መንገሥት በዐፄ ሱሰኔስ ዘመተዉ ምእት ዓመት እዳ የናፈዉና ጋሳ ብሎ የሚታዩ ኢትዮጵያዊ ፈላስፋ) አንደጸፈዉ:: "ተፈጥሮቿን የሚያዛን የአመና የጠጣ አንደንመገብ ነዉ::"

የፈላስፋዉ ዘርዐ ያዕቆብ ደቀ መዝሙር ወልደ ሕይወት በጽሑፉ አንደለፈረዉ:: "አሕይወትሁ የሚጠጠቀሙሁን ምግቦቿ ምረጥ በጥንቃቄ በጥበብና በአጽሕናም አዘጋጃቸዉ:: አንደጣፈጡሁና ሕይወትም አንደሁሩህ አገዚአብሔር ለዚህ ልቦና ሰጥተሃል::"

ZARA YAËCOB (THE FIRST ETHIOPIAN PHILOSOPHER, DURING ATSE SUSUNIOS DYNASTY, 17TH CENTURY) WROTE "NATURE ORDERS US TO EAT FINE AND TASTY FOOD…," WHILE HIS DISCIPLE WOLDE-HIWOT TRANSCRIBED "CHOOSE THE BEST MEALS, PREPARE THEM CAREFULLY, SKILLFULLY, AND CLEANLY. GOD GAVE YOU THE WISDOM TO PREPARE MEALS THAT ARE TASTY ENOUGH TO FEED YOUR SOUL."

It is said that the Queen of Sheba, Nigist Makeda, visited King Solomon bearing gold, precious stones, and spices. The Books of Chronicles in the Old Testament documents this, commenting that "Never again came such an abundance of spice" (10:10; II Chron. 9:1-9) as those our Queen gave to the King. Gold remains a valuable currency today, yet among all the gifts she offered, only the spices were mentioned as objects of attention that even the Wise Ruler never saw again.

Food is an object of survival, an entity believed to feed the body and soul across different cultures around the world. In Ethiopia on the other hand, it holds another crucial dimension, one that conveys a positive human energy through a powerful saying "enebla." *Enebla*, in Amharic, translates to "let us eat" and our staple food *injera* is made in a way that invites more than one hand to the meal. It is a moment of sharing, of caring, and of showing respect for one another.

Through the numerous dynasties and civilizations that surfaced and vanished across this land, meals have always been at the core of them all. This passion and worth we attribute to food has allowed our crafts to sharpen beyond imagination. With more than 3,000 years of culinary legacy, we continue to treasure these gastronomic gifts, and today, I am honored to share the mysteries of their confection to the world and to you on behalf of those who worked hard to preserve them.

From *berbere*, the spice blend that takes more than three days to achieve complexity within heat, to *injera*, our gluten-free daily teff flatbread, which also requires three moons to acquire the perfect elasticity and taste, and of course let us not forget coffee, the country's first culinary gift to the world, this book will open your eyes to culinary wonders from Ethiopia, the Land of Origins.

Born in Addis Ababa, Ethiopia, I grew up in a typical Ethiopian family where traditional ceremonies and social events like *Mahber* (community bonding celebrations) were broadly practiced. Whenever festivities came around I used to follow my mother in the kitchen while she prepared a large pot of *niter kebbeh* (Ethiopian spiced clarified butter), which flavored all the delicious meals for the guests we would welcome. As a young boy, then as tall as the kitchen table, I couldn't observe all the spices that were added but I could smell each of them and, as greedy as I am for such sublime aromatic beauty, I would walk all day next to her, holding her dress, eyes closed and my nose raised to the ceiling.

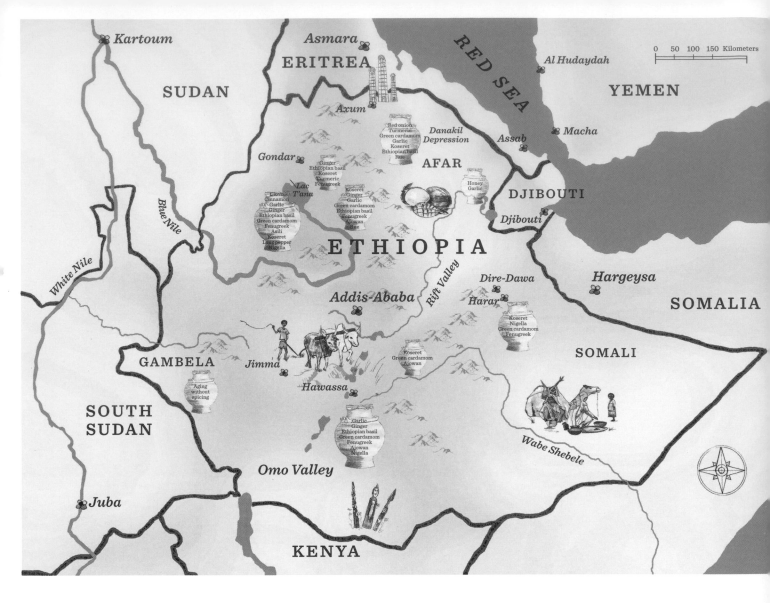

Passionate about art in all its forms, I eventually ventured into the culinary arts industry by studying at the Paul Bocuse Institute and fine-dining restaurants in the southern cities of France, which ultimately allowed me to see food as more than just an interest. On one hand I witnessed a science that requires the utmost precision, and on the other, I developed a keen curiosity for discovering new tastes. This education allowed me to travel to the four corners of the world, including a hands-on experience in a Californian luxury resort. It made me realize how much I still had to learn, but more importantly, that it was finally time to go back to my origins, in order to unfold the rich culture I am proud to be part of.

Returning to Addis Ababa, I worked on a TV show entitled "Chef Yohanis Qegnet"—a 30-minute culinary and lifestyle entertainment show that took me all over Ethiopia, traveling across the country. By meeting people from the 80 different ethnic groups throughout the country, and sharing bread with each family, I was able to discover the culinary jewels and various processes of each region. I've grown to believe that this interaction with every part of my country is my path to fully discovering who I am. It's given me a glimpse of the abundance of Ethiopian cuisine and the ceaseless teachings that built the key foundations of my ancestors' lives.

Indeed, Ethiopia is one of the countries in the world whose pride is established on a lengthy and rich history. Situated in the horn of Africa, next to Sudan and Eritrea, it is the source of the Blue Nile, one of the two major tributaries of the River Nile. As part of the Nile countries, early Ethiopian history can be traced to more than 2000 BC as Abyssinia, the land of mixed races, and to having a strong relationship with Egypt during the Six Dynasty. The few old Ethiopian inscriptions from the pagan time claim Pharaohs of the Old Kingdom were kings of the two lands that in the beginning were one.

While very few traces from our pagan history remain—like the obelisks of *Axum,* the name of my childhood best friend, Meherem, or the Ethiopian version of Mars the War God—our history, and consequently our cuisine, is mainly shaped alongside Christianity. Following a close full millennia of Judaism, brought to Ethiopia with Nigist Makeda and her son Menelik I, allegedly the offspring of King Solomon, Christianity ruled.

The Ethiopian Orthodox Tewahedo church was first officially recognized when King Ezana first adopted the faith, and it has influenced our political, cultural, and social life until recent years. This influence is easily identified in our cuisine via the numerous vegetarian recipes prepared during fasting seasons, a serious obligation for half a year, every year. By contrast, Islam arrived in Ethiopia during *Hijrah*—the migration—through the disciples of Prophet Mohammed. Today, a third of the country is Muslim and the religion has molded the social life of several regions, including but not limited to, Somali, Afar, Argobba, Harar, Dire Dawa, and Alaba. Islam played a crucial role in introducing sweets to the plethora of our meals. Sweets like halawa and *mushebak* are widely available in Dire-Dawa and Harar. Then again, the culture of eating sweets regularly did not expand throughout Ethiopia, perhaps because their confection still remains a secret known only by harari families who make and sell them.

Ethiopia is large, about twice the size of France, and the country's cuisine is also influenced by its different climates and geography. From the Denakil Depression of Afar situated 410 feet below sea level, to the two-third of the country's plateaus ranging from 4,000 to 10,000 feet, the landscapes greatly influence its cuisines based on the ingredients each region can produce and the know-how of communities required to survive there. Whether it's the use of goat skin to naturally cool water in very hot regions of Afar, the burning of specific plants to extract edible salt in Gambela, or Aja Kita whistling—the art of using sound vibration in Lalibela—Ethiopia is home to limitless ingenuity.

Trading with far Asia and the Middle East, especially Yemen, as well as the various battles across our history—including the one with Italy and its four years of occupation in 1935—are also factors that have shaped our cuisine. Yet, never colonized, Ethiopia's culinary and cultural diversity is a point of pride to the continent, and is always ready to share its crafts with anyone who listens.

Today, I genuinely believe that it is time for Ethiopian food to be made globally available, and for the tastes and health benefits to be celebrated. My ambition is for our learnings to serve as a ground of exploration for others. In a world where traditions are kneeling to faster paced, industrialized lifestyles, only by making time for the simple pleasures in life can we nurture the intangible jewels that were left gracefully to us by former generations. Learning from one another can provide a healthier, globally abundant, and tastier world for us all. It would at least, undoubtedly, allow our palates to unravel their true potential to appreciate an endless variety of worldwide cuisine.

Join me now while I guide you through the Ethiopian landscape, on the plot where Lucy "Denkenesh" carved her home, on the spread where Nigist Makeda harvested her spices, on the parcel of land where Kaldi first witnessed his goats eating coffee beans and where they all shared *injera*, across time and space, with one constant: a warm, generous, and genuine Ethiopian hospitality.

Before turning on the stove

Spices and heat

Just as every palate is different, so is every spice blend, and therefore it is hard to give precise amounts for certain key ingredients. The fiery *mitmita* (see page 47), for instance, is generally intended as a seasoning to be added gradually, tasting as you go. This technique, however, doesn't work as well with the ubiquitous *berbere* (see page 40) which flavors and colors all of our red stews. *Berbere* needs to be cooked to lose its intense heat and dusty taste. The amount I include in a recipe is therefore a minimum suggestion and so it's a good idea to experiment to find what is right for your palate and to use more (or less), as desired.

Ethiopian ingredients, substitutions, and tools

The less common spices called for in these recipes—ajowan and nigella, for instance—should be readily available in well-stocked spice shops. Certain specific Ethiopian ingredients require more effort to locate, although most can be found on the internet from specialist retailers. Cities with large Ethiopian diaspora have small Ethiopian grocery stores that carry essential ingredients such as *niter kebbeh*, dry *shiro*

flours, *tej*, *koseret* and other herbs, and the main spice blends, including *berbere*. Many also sell fresh *injera*. Also, check Ethiopian restaurants, as they often stock some grocery items and sell *injera* to go.

Tej

Fermented honey wine is a popular indigenous drink of Ethiopia and is found in a number of our traditional recipes and in some of my modern versions. While certainly not the easiest item to locate outside Ethiopia—made even more difficult by the lack of many commercial brands—it is easy to substitute. Simply whisk 1 tablespoon of honey into 1 cup (250 ml) of dry white wine.

Mitad

There are very few specialist tools required in the Ethiopian kitchen. However, the notable exception is the *mitad*, a large, round griddle, often up to 24 inches (60 cm) in diameter. Made of highly polished clay and with a dome lid, it is used for cooking *injera* and other flatbreads. However, if you can't track one down online, use a large, non-stick crêpe pan, frying pan,

or griddle. *Mitad* is also the name given to the iron griddle used to roast coffee beans in the traditional Ethiopian coffee ceremony.

Electric grinder

An electric spice or coffee grinder is extremely useful for grinding spices and flaxseed, and also for making *beso*, a flour made from roasted barley that is hard to buy outside of Ethiopia.

Kulet

Nearly every stewed dish (also called "*Wot*") in the Ethiopian repertoire calls for *kulet*—often lots of it. *Kulet* consists mainly of three ingredients: finely chopped red onion, grated garlic, and ginger. While the quantities of each ingredient can vary depending on the recipe, in *kulet* you are required to cook the chopped onion first, without any oil, until soft and almost dry. Only then do we add the garlic and ginger along with the oil until the mix caramelizes and becomes *kulet*. During the non-fasting season a spoon of *niter kebbeh* (see page 52) is also added in the making and scenting of *kulet*. Its sweetness through slow-cooking and the caramelization process balances the spices, giving texture and body to sauces that use it as a base. Be patient when chopping; the sauce should be quite smooth rather than chunky. Shallots are prized for their flavor and were the most dominant ingredient in markets during my childhood, but today cooks generally use red onions, which are less laborious to peel and chop. For smaller quantities of *kulet*, the recipes in this book use oil to avoid burning the onion mix.

Spelling

Ethiopia mostly uses Amharic as a spoken language, although numerous languages exist and are actively practiced all around the country. Amharic comes from Geez, a Semitic language with its own alphabets, and where some alphabets have their own unique resonance compared to Latin languages. Thus, there is no standard translation of Amharic words into English. For example, there seems to be a dozen ways to write our ubiquitous spiced clarified butter, from *niter kebbeh* to *nit'ir qibe*. In continued efforts to be loyal to the pronunciation of certain culinary words, the spellings used throughout this book were chosen according to the most faithful to the correct sounds and most commonly used translations.

Injera &
Flatbreads

1

Teff

The high central plateau that covers much of Ethiopia is a place of open skies. Humped Zebu till the land with wooden ploughs, raptors glide on updrafts above flat-topped mountains, and breezes send shimmying ripples across fields of wispy green stalks. However, it isn't wheat that grows so profusely here—this is teff country.

Held in the hand, the tiny grains of this indigenous cereal (first domesticated by Ethiopians some 3,000 years ago) are sandy, about the size of poppyseeds. There are 3,000 of them in a single gram[1] (the same number of wheat grains weigh 195 grams), yet each one is a dense powerhouse of nutrients: iron, fiber, calcium, and protein.

Teff is Ethiopia's most widely farmed crop, grown by an estimated 6.5 million Ethiopian farmers and, especially in the highlands, retains an incomparable importance. It also accounts for around 15 percent of the country's total calories since *injera*,[2] our staple food (see pages 20–25)—a spongy, tart flatbread made from teff—is, literally, the base of most meals: food is placed directly on it instead of a plate.

In fact, so key is teff to Ethiopia that our government prohibits its export in grain form. At the moment, only teff that has been milled into flour can be exported. However, many outside Ethiopia have discovered teff's nutritional potential and the fact that it is gluten-free also heightens its current popularity. Growing awareness and demand have led to cultivation elsewhere. Today, teff grows in several regions of the US, Canada, India, Australia, and parts of Europe. There are three main types of teff: ivory, dark brown, and light brown, the latter referred to as *key*, meaning "red" in Amharic. Ivory, considered the highest quality, has the mildest flavor, and dark brown variety is the most popular and commonly available teff for making *injera*.

In order to develop the elasticity needed to make spongy *injera*, the batter has to be fermented. With a sourdough-like starter, it is left to ferment for three days before an additional step called *absit* happens. *Absit* is a distinctive Ethiopian cooking technique that requires boiling some of the batter then, while hot, stirring it back into the initial starter. This process allows to speed up the fermentation process and favor

an enhanced spongy texture for *injera*. This lends it its signature tartness and spongy texture—a flavor that acts as a perfect foil for the boldly flavored stews it accompanies.

In Ethiopia's various traditions, only a few recipes require the use of wooden forks, like *tihelo* in Tigray, and the use of spoons made of oxen horns— like the *Guragué kitfo* or the *genfos* (thick porridges) of *Oromia* and *Gambela* for instance. Undeniably, *injera*, aside from being food itself, serves as the perfect combination of all utensils. Some people refer our skills of manipulating *injera* as "dancing with fingers." Eating with *injera* demands washing properly first—via a traditional water pot and bucket, brought to guests at the dining table. Having said grace, guests are invited to break pieces of *injera* using only the right hand. They apply the flatbread over the stews while avoiding covering their nails with the liquids, then dipping and rolling it, to form a *"goursha"*—an *injera* bite that combines all the stews from the platter.

Most of our recipes are stews, which means the spongy texture of *injera* is a defining aspect when assesing the quality. And, just like steak needs a sharp knife to cut it, Ethiopian stews require *injera* to have the maximum quantity and quality of holes, known as *"ayen."* *Ayen* in Amharic means "eye," in reference to the shattered air bubbles on top of *ingera* during baking. These holes carve its spongy texture, enabling it to absorb the sauce.

Such is the reason why mixing *ingera* batter and baking it is a very difficult task that takes cooks many years to master. Baking *injera* requires layering the batter in a spiral direction on *mitad*, clockwise for right-handed cooks and counter-clockwise for lefties. By having the layers just touch, *injera* becomes very thin, ultimately maximizing its flexibility so the flatbread doesn't break when clamping chunks, and at the same time creating consistent-sized *ayen* that soak up lots of sauce.

1. www.teffco.com/what-is-teff

2. Anahad O'Connor (2016) "Is Teff the New Super Grain?" *The New York Times* Available at https://well.blogs.nytimes.com/2016/08/16/is-teff-the-new-super-grain

Traditional Injera

*If you are starting from scratch, making traditional **injera** takes a week, since you need four days to make the sponge (starter) plus another three to prepare the batter. However, the first step need only be done once, as a cup of the batter is then used as a starter for the next batch and so on and so forth. If pressed for time, you can also skip the sponge step (see recipe for One-day Injera, page 24), and while the injera might lack a little authentic flavor, the next batch will regain it, if you save some of the batter to use the next time. Use bottled water, since the chlorine found in tap water may interfere with the natural fermentation process.*

*   **Injera** is not cooked as crêpes are, by tilting the pan quickly to make the pancake even or by spreading out with a tool. Instead, it is poured in a stream in a spiral manner, starting at the outside edge of the pan towards the center. The lines of batter should just meet, without any overlap or gaps. There is a real art to cooking **injera**, and it takes a lot of practice to be able to achieve perfect rounds. But it will still be delicious either way.*

**MAKES 7–9 MEDIUM
OR 5 LARGE *INJERA***

6½ cups (1 lb 10 oz/750 g) teff flour
    (see note, right)
7 cups (1.65 liters) bottled water,
    plus more as needed
vegetable oil for oiling pan

Day 1

Begin by making a sponge or yeast starter: In a large non-reactive bowl or plastic jug with a lid, sift a generous 2 cups (9 oz/250 g) of the flour and, using your hands, begin slowly working in about 1 cup (250 ml) of water until you have a very moist, squishy dough without any lumps—it should take about 5 minutes. Pour over ½ cup (125 ml) water so that the mixture is entirely submerged, then tightly cover and let it rest for four days at room temperature.

Day 4

The mixture will have separated into two layers: a thick, yeasty sponge on the bottom and a watery layer on the top. Carefully pour off and discard the watery top layer so that only the sponge underneath remains. You will need only a portion of this sponge to progress. You can use the leftover sponge to make successive batches of *injera*; it will keep, covered in the refrigerator, for several days.

In a large non-reactive bowl, measure out 1 cup (250 ml) of the sponge. Using your hands, mix in the remaining 4⅓ cups (1 lb 2 oz/500 g) of flour and ½ cup (125 ml) of water. When you start smelling a pleasantly sour aroma, gradually add a generous 1½ cups (375 ml) of water. Once the mixture is smooth, with no lumps, pour about 1⅔ cups (400 ml) of water on top; do not stir in this layer of water. Cover tightly and let the mixture rest for three days at room temperature.

Day 7

After three days, remove the lid and take a look. The batter may bubble and smell sour—these are good signs. However, if you see any bits of mold develop on the surface, scoop out and discard. Pour off and discard the watery liquid layer on top and reserve what is left: this is the base batter.

Make the *absit*. In a large saucepan, bring 1 cup (250 ml) of water to a boil. Whisk in ½ cup (125 ml) of the base batter and ½ cup (125 ml) of water. When this mixture begins to thicken and bubble, remove it from the heat. It should have the consistency of thin cooked oatmeal. Let it cool to just warm. This mixture is called *absit*.

Mix the *absit* into the bowl with the base batter to create a final batter. The mixture should have a consistency mid-way between a crêpe and pancake batter. If it is too thick, stir in a little additional room-temperature water. Cover the bowl with a dish towel and let it rest for about 2 hours, until bubbles have begun to form on the surface. The bubbles are the sign that the final fermentation has occurred and that the *injera* batter is ready to be cooked.

Cooking the *injera*

To cook the *injera*, use a non-stick crêpe pan or skillet, or large, traditional *mitad*. Moisten a paper towel with oil and wipe the surface, then place the pan over medium–high heat.

When the pan is hot, use a spouted measuring cup to scoop ½–1 cup (125–250 ml) of the batter, depending on the size of the pan (a standard 11 inch/28 cm crêpe pan will take about ¾ cup/175 ml of batter). For a large *mitad*, use about twice as much batter. Work quickly and carefully in order to pour the batter evenly around the pan. Starting at the outside edge of the cooking surface—going clockwise if you are right-handed or counterclockwise if you are left-handed—pour the batter in a thin stream and in one continuous motion in a spiral formation, without overlapping, until you end at the very center. There might be some batter left over in the scoop. While not traditional, if using a crêpe pan, swirl the pan if needed to evenly distribute the batter.

Cook undisturbed until bubbles have begun to form on the surface of the *injera* and the batter begins to set. When about 75 percent of the surface batter has changed color, 45 seconds–1½ minutes, cover the pan with a large lid. (A glass lid is helpful here as it allows you to check the doneness of the *injera* without uncovering.) Cook until the edges of the *injera* begin to curl, the top is quite dry, and the *injera* has released from the bottom of the pan, from 30 seconds–1½ minutes (it might be longer with a larger *mitad*). Do not flip the *injera*.

When cooked, use a long thin spatula and a thin plate or piece of cardboard to transfer the *injera* to a flat basket or a large plate lined with parchment paper without breaking.

Remove any stray dough from the cooking surface, and then apply more oil as necessary and reheat. (After the first few *injera*, lower the heat to medium–low.) Continue making them in the same way, layering each *injera* on top of the last on the basket or plate as they are finished. Allow to cool for at least 5 minutes before placing another on top, and allow all to rest for at least 30 minutes before serving. Cover any leftovers loosely with plastic wrap and they will keep for about 2 days.

Note: There are a few different types of teff flour. The most common to use for *injera* are ivory and brown.

One-Day Injera

*While purists might balk at calling this **injera**, this quick version can be made in just a day. This recipe is adapted from the Ethiopian-owned company WASS Electronics in the US that makes **mitads**—the round griddles—for preparing **injera**. The company sells to the Ethiopian community in North America and Europe, and to Ethiopian restaurants who want to replicate the authentic experience. There are plenty of coveted eyes (**ayen**) on the surface; a hint of sourness, an important key to balancing the flavors the stews; and a spongy, chewy texture.*

If you are in a rush, you can prepare this recipe without letting it sit overnight. It won't have that slight sour taste, but the texture will be similar.

*This recipe makes about 3 cups (700 ml) of batter, enough for roughly 2 large (16 inch/40 cm) or 3 to 4 medium (10 inch/25 cm) **injera**. Double the quantities if desired. A standard 11 inch (28 cm) crêpe pan is ideal for preparing this recipe.*

SERVES 2

2 cups (8½ oz/240 g) teff flour
(see page 21)

2 cups (500 ml) bottled water

¼ teaspoon salt

½ tablespoon baking powder

vegetable oil for oiling pan

In a large non-reactive bowl, add the flour and begin working in the water. Stir well. Cover with a dish towel and let sit undisturbed on the kitchen counter for 24 hours.

After this period, the batter should be slightly foamy. Whisk in the salt and the baking powder. (The batter will deflate as you stir.)

Cook the *injera* following the directions on page 21.

Thin Flat Oat Cakes

From the countryside of Lalibela come these thin flat cakes made from oat flour. The
ayen—*"eyes"—or bubbles on the surface give them a lovely supple sponginess and, in order*
to help create these bubbles, children gather around the griddle to whistle directly at the
cooking batter. The vibrations help the **ayen** *to form on the surface.*
   Aja kita is most often served as part of a **buna kurs,** *"coffee breakfast."*

In a large mixing bowl, sift the flour and begin whisking in 2–2 ½ cups (500–600 ml) of lukewarm water until foamy. The mixture should have the consistency of thick pancake batter.

Heat a large griddle or frying pan over medium heat. Moisten some paper towels with oil and carefully wipe the pan. Working in batches, ladle in just enough batter to coat the pan, tilting the pan if needed to evenly coat the base.

SERVES 4

generous 2 cups (8 oz/225 g) oat flour
flaxseed flour or vegetable oil, for
   dusting or oiling the pan

Cook while whistling directly onto the batter. Once bubbles appear, cover with a large lid and cook for 5 minutes, then flip and cook, covered, for another 1–2 minutes until done. Be careful not to overcook—the final consistency should be spongy. Remove from the griddle and either serve immediately or keep warm while you cook the remaining batter.

Whole-Grain Bread Baked in Banana Leaves

*This whole-grain bread is always part of the festive table. It is baked wrapped in **enset** leaves (see page 30) or banana leaves, and this both keeps it spongy and lends it a lovely fruitiness (look for banana leaves in Asian groceries). **Dabo** means bread, while **defo**—"to drop"—refers to how the moist, sticky dough is tipped or poured from the bowl into a mold. Because the dough rises and pulls away from some of the leaves as it bakes, cover the mold with foil to ensure the dough remains protected.*

*There is also a similar bread called **mulmul dabo** that uses smaller pieces of dough wrapped in **enset** leaves and baked. These are a favorite for the Buhe holiday in August, which celebrates the transfiguration of Jesus on Mount Tabor. During this colorful festivity, children gather sticks that are then lit with families while dancing and chanting.*

MAKES 1 LARGE LOAF

6¼ cups (1 lb 10 oz/750 g) wholewheat flour

2¼ teaspoons active dry yeast
(one ¼ oz/7g envelope)

½ teaspoon nigella seeds

¼ teaspoon ground ajowan

1 teaspoon salt

1½ tablespoons sunflower, canola, or another
mild vegetable oil

fresh banana leaves, for wrapping

3 garlic cloves, peeled

Sift the flour into a large mixing bowl. Add the yeast, nigella seeds, ajowan, salt, and oil, and mix by hand. Begin working in about 2 cups (500 ml) of warm water until the dough is smooth but also quite sticky. Cover with plastic wrap and leave to rise for 1 hour.

Preheat the oven to 400°F (200°C). Line a deep round ovensafe mold or Dutch oven with banana leaves and tip in the dough. Insert the garlic cloves evenly across the top and tuck the banana leaves around the dough until it is completely covered. Wrap the top of the mold in foil.

Bake for 45–60 minutes or until cooked; it should sound hollow when tapped. Once cool, carefully pull away the banana leaves and cut into quarters.

Enset

The highway south from Addis Ababa drops down off the high plateau into the parched Rift Valley and follows a string of small soda lakes, which are home to abundant wildlife and the source of much of the country's fish. The road passes through the town of Shashemene, known for its Rastafarian community—Emperor Haile Selassie's pre-coronation name was Ras Tefari and followers of this religious movement believe him to be the Messiah—and then Hawassa, the Rift Valley's largest city.

Beyond Hawassa, the road climbs up out of starkness and dry heat, and the land quickly begins to breathe with dozens of shades of green—this is the hallowed coffee-producing land of Sidamo and Yirgacheffee. The soil turns crimson and charcoal afternoon clouds often threaten rain. Huddled around beehive-shaped huts are Arabica coffee trees, garden crops, and tall *enset* trees with dark, peeling trunks and giant, blade-shaped leaves.

While teff is the undisputed highland staple (see pages 16–17), in the south and west of the country it is *enset*. Endemic to the region, it has been cultivated for some 7,000 years[1] and for some 18–20 million people—about 20 percent of Ethiopia's population[2]—it forms the backbone of their diet.

Enset is known as "the tree against hunger" for its resistance to drought—it can supposedly survive for seven years without rain. It requires little upkeep and, unlike most other staple crops, can be harvested throughout the year.

Enset looks like a banana tree but it bears no fruit—hence its moniker "false banana." Rather, *enset's* starchy pulp gets scraped out and squeezed in cloth. The dripping liquid is dried to become *bula*, a starchy gelatin used in the making of *bula genfo*, a type of thick breakfast porridge (see page 58). Young stems are also chopped, boiled, and eaten like vegetables, and its leaves have a multitude of uses in the kitchen. For baking, cooks wrap them around leavened bread dough to impart a fruitiness to the loaf while keeping it moist and spongy. Merchants at local markets fold them into simple wrappers for butter, fresh cheese, and coffee beans, while, in the Guragé culture, it's also used as an eco-friendly plate to serve *kitfo*, seasoned raw ground beef (see page 144).

Enset's most famous culinary use, though, is to make *kocho*, my dad's favorite childhood root bread. Preparing *kocho* demands great leg flexibility to be able to harvest the pulpy mass of starch from the *enset* roots and branches. The starch is scraped off the tree, then gathered together, wrapped in leaves, buried underground, and left for several weeks—or even several years—to ferment, before it's taken out and baked as a bread on *mitad*. *Kocho* accompanies fresh cheese, cabbage, and meat dishes, such as *kitfo,* during a typical day.

For many in the south and west of Ethiopia, *enset* is more than just an important part of their diet. Its cultural significance runs deep. In some origin stories, the first person to appear on the Earth carried *enset*—a gift from the gods.[3] It has been nourishing people there ever since.

---

1. Rachel Stern (2015) "Faced with climate change, Ethiopia rediscovers an ancient staple crop," *Deutsche Welle*. Available at http://www.dw.com/en/ethiopia-rediscovers-ancient-staple-crop/a-18823060

2. *Ibid.*

3. Werner J. Lange *History of the Southern Gonga* (Steiner, 1982), p.180. "Manjo and Matto came out of a hole in the earth near Shadda. They were both naked as they came out of the earth. They had nothing on them. Matto brought ensete and a potato, which were given to him by the god to bring him out of the hole. One steer and one cow also came out of the hole with Matto [...]"

Round Flatbread

This round, griddle-baked bread from northern Ethiopia is easily identified by the spiderweb-like design across its top. Loved for its crispy roasted crust and moist, crumby interior with hints of nigella, it is broken at the beginning of a meal to serve as an appetizer and, after the meal, as a "closer." It also goes nicely with coffee.

The key to a successful loaf is to lay the dough evenly over a griddle or large frying pan. When one side is cooked, use a rolling mat or large plate to help flip it over without breaking, ensuring the other side is laid evenly onto the griddle to cook.

Sift the flour into a large mixing bowl. Add the yeast, nigella seeds, and salt and mix by hand. Begin working in about 1 cup (250 ml) of warm water until you have a firm but not stiff dough, adding a touch more water if required. Knead for about 5 minutes until smooth, then rub a little oil on the bottom and place in a large bowl. Cover with a moist dish towel and leave for 1–2 hours until it has doubled in size.

Transfer the dough to a lightly floured rolling mat and gently work the dough with your fingers, stretching it into a wide disc about 12 inches (30 cm) across and ³/₄–1 inch (2–2.5 cm) thick. Set aside to rest for a few minutes before using the tip of a sharp knife to score a spiderweb design across the top. Gently dimple the edges with your fingertips. Traditionally, the design is specific to Christianity and begins by making a cross first then adding the rest of the patterns.

MAKES 1 LARGE LOAF

4 cups (1 lb 2 oz/500 g) all-purpose flour, plus extra for dusting

2¼ teaspoons active dry yeast (one ¼ oz/7g envelope)

½ teaspoon nigella seeds

1 teaspoon salt

olive oil, for moistening the bread

Heat a large griddle or a 12–14 inch (30–35 cm) frying pan over medium heat. Reduce the heat to medium–low and, with the help of the rolling mat, gently place the bread onto the pan, design-side down. Cover with a dome-shaped lid (or sheets of foil) and cook for 10 minutes until the crust is crispy and golden. Flip and cook for about 10 minutes on the other side. When ready, the loaf should make a somewhat hollow sound when tapped. Cook for a couple of minutes more on each side if needed.

Transfer to a plate, design-side up, and lightly rub the top with oil before serving.

Spicy Shepherds' Bread

Around the country, there are a number of dense, griddle-baked flatbreads that workers or shepherds take with them to sustain them through a day's work. Many different types of flour are used—wheat, but also barley, corn, sorghum, teff, and millet. The spicy **torosho** comes from Debra Birhan and Ankobar in the mountainous Amhara region north of Addis Ababa. There is small kick of **berbere** spice in the bread, a flavor especially appreciated by the shepherds who graze their flocks along the area's chilly, thyme-scented slopes.

The bread is unleavened and unrested; the dough is formed, quickly decorated with a wheat grain-like pattern, and immediately cooked on the **mitad** or large, round griddle. Washing the flour off towards the end of cooking and then returning to the griddle changes the final texture and gives a lovely, slightly glossy smoothness to the crust.

MAKES 1 SMALL LOAF

2¼ cups (10 oz/275 g) all-purpose flour, plus extra for dusting

1 teaspoon sunflower, canola, or other mild vegetable oil

1 tablespoon berbere spice blend (page 40)

1 teaspoon sugar

1 teaspoon salt

Sift the flour into a large mixing bowl. Add the oil, berbere, sugar, and salt, and begin working in about ¾ cup (175 ml) of warm water. Mix by hand until elastic, adding a touch more water if needed. The dough shouldn't be sticky. Do not rest the dough.

Sprinkle a generous amount of flour over a rolling mat or clean surface and, with your fingertips, press the dough out into a round about 12 inches (30 cm) across and ½ inch (1 cm) thick. Using a sharp knife blade, decorate the top with a zigzag pattern.

Heat a large griddle over medium heat. Gently lay the dough over the griddle and cook for 2 minutes, then flip and cook for a further 2 minutes.

Using wet hands, wipe off the excess flour. Return the bread to the griddle and cook for another 1–2 minutes on each side until done. The loaf should be dry but not brittle so be careful not to overcook it.

Shiro Sliders with Fresh Sausage

*Made from a blend of dried legumes and spices, **shiro** flour is one of the most important and common ingredients in the Ethiopian kitchen. And if you dust it onto dough when making bread it creates a delightful powdery crust, with hints of our local spice box.*

SERVES 6–8

2¾ cups (12 oz/350 g) all-purpose flour

1 teaspoon salt

1 teaspoon instant yeast

mitten shiro flour (page 103), for dusting

1 lb 5 oz (600 g) fresh spicy merguez sausages, preferably in links

cherry tomatoes, halved, to garnish

sweet fresh basil leaves, to garnish

For the spicy aioli

1 egg yolk

1 garlic clove, mashed

a dollop of mustard

¾ cup (175 ml) olive oil

a pinch of chopped chives

mitmita spice blend (page 47)

salt and freshly ground black pepper

In a large mixing bowl, sift the flour and salt. Add the yeast and about 1 cup (240 ml) of water. With your hands, mix well and then knead for about 5 minutes into a firm but not stiff dough. Add a touch more flour or drops of water if needed—the dough should be smooth and tacky but not sticky.

Sprinkle a clean work surface with *shiro* flour. Divide the dough in half and shape each half into a long, thin loaf. Dust with *shiro*, then place on a baking tray, cover with a dish towel, and let rise for 45 minutes.

Preheat the oven to 400°F (200°C).

Once the dough has risen, score the surface of each loaf diagonally 3–4 times. Bake, rotating the pan halfway through, for 20–30 minutes until done—the loaves should sound hollow when tapped. Remove from the oven and set aside to cool.

Prepare the aioli. In a mixing bowl, whisk together the egg yolk, garlic, and mustard. When the mixture has some body, slowly whisk in the oil in a thin, continuous drizzle. When all of oil has been incorporated into an emulsion, fold in the chives and season with *mitmita*, salt ,and pepper. Cover and refrigerate until ready to use.

Preheat your grill or broiler and, when hot, grill the sausages.

Slice the bread and generously spread with aioli. Fill each sandwich with sausages, tomatoes, and basil and serve.

2

Seasonings

Ethiopian Spice Box

While Merkato might be the most famous market in Addis Ababa and supposedly the largest open-air one in Africa, people also head to Shola market on the northeast side of the city when they want to buy *qemam*, spices for cooking. These are the main herbs and spices we go to buy:

Ajowan or bishop's weed (*nech azmud*): While these tiny, ridged and tear-shaped seeds are closely related to cumin and caraway—the Amharic name means "white cumin"; we commonly call them "Ethiopian caraway"—their taste is closer to dried thyme. Ajowan is nearly always added to a dish in ground form. (Latin: *Trachyspermum ammi*) Substitute: a combination of dried thyme and cumin seeds.

Besobela: Commonly known as holy or sacred basil and sometimes called "Ethiopian basil," the fragrant, purple-blossomed herb is a key ingredient in *berbere*. Although the leaves look more like lavender flowers, the flavor is quite similar to Thai basil. (Latin: *Ocimum tenuiflorum*) Substitute: dried Thai basil.

Black pepper (*kundo berbere*): While not generally a table condiment in Ethiopia, some people use black pepper for seasoning during cooking.

Cloves (*krenfud*): Found in the finishing spice blend *mekelesha* (see page 44), these dried, unopened flower buds exude a warm, aromatic sweetness and are locally used as traditional medicine, especially in spiced teas known as *kimen shai*.

Coriander (*dimbilal*): Hinting of anise and lemons, these pale brown seeds are occasionally found in some *niter kebbeh*, spice blends, and mild sauces.

Cumin: There are two types of cumin available in local markets—the local variety and one imported from the Middle East. Both are used in the making of specific Ethiopian recipes.

Fenugreek (*abish*): Mustard-brown, pebble-hard seeds, sharp and pungent with a nuttiness and hints of burnt sugar when toasted. *Abish* is key to certain stews, especially in eastern Ethiopia and specifically Harar (see page 132). Locally, it is never used freshly ground, instead washed several times then malted and powdered. This reduces the bitterness. Make sure to consider this factor when preparing recipes that use *abish*.

Garlic (*nech shinkurt*): Widely paired with ginger in the *kulet* base of many stews, garlic is an essential ingredient. The Amharic name literally translates to "white onion."

Ginger (*zinjibel*): Found in many dishes, fresh ginger often gets added with garlic in *kulet*, although some *kulet* does not include it. Traditionally, it is peeled and mashed in a mortar, but an easier and more effective technique is to wash it thoroughly, freeze it, and then grate the ginger directly into the sauce when needed.

Korerima: The local version of grains of paradise, or malagueta pepper, has a less pungent bite and more sweet cardamom-like aromas than the ones from the humid, tropical coast of West Africa that dominate the international market. Grown in the heavy shade of Ethiopia's southern forests, *korerima* pods are the size and shape of figs but a tinny-grey color. While the shape of *korerima* is identical to grains of paradise, the local version on the other hand is identical in aroma and taste to the green cardamom. Substitute: green cardamom.

Koseret: This shrubby, oregano-like indigenous herb from the verbena family is most famously used in spicing clarified butter, *niter kebbeh*. This ingredient is challenging to substitute as its aroma is unique and very pronounced when added to *niter kebbeh* and to all the major Ethiopian Spice blends. (Latin: *Lippia abyssinica*) Substitute: dried oregano.

Long pepper (*timiz*): Grown in the southern highland forests, these cylindrical spikes have a citrusy tang to their peppery bite. (Latin: *Piper capense*) Substitute: black pepper.

Nigella sativa (*tikur azmud*): Also called "black cumin"—*tikur* means black in Amharic—these matte black seeds have a mild, earthy flavor with peppery notes. They are generally added whole to breads and ground to stews. Substitute: cumin seeds combined with black pepper.

Rue or herb of grace (*tena adam*): This herb, locally used for its unique flavor and medicinal properties, gives a slightly bitter freshness to spice blends, fresh milk, and yogurt, and garnishes cups of coffee. Substitute: for spice blends, use a smaller amount of cilantro and lemon zest to bring a touch of freshness.

Tosegn: An aromatic, native variety of wild lemon thyme. Substitute: dried lemon thyme.

Turmeric (*ird*): In addition to its health benefits, this dried and ground rhizome gives onion-rich *alicha* stews their signature golden color and some woody, earthy notes.

Berbere Spice Blend

Integral to Ethiopian cuisine, this chili-based spice blend gives countless dishes not only heat and flavor but also their signature rich, dark red color. Traditionally, it takes a number of days to complete the entire process of preparing **berbere** *(see page 42) and so Ethiopian households often make it in vast quantities only a couple of times a year. However, this is an easy version that can be put together quickly so scale up as desired.*

**MAKES A GENEROUS ½ CUP
(2 oz/55 g)**

1 ¾ oz (50 g) dried medium-hot red chilies, such
    as guajillo or New Mexico chilies (about 10)

½ teaspoon nigella seeds

½ teaspoon cloves

½ teaspoon ajowan seeds

½ tablespoon onion powder

1 teaspoon garlic powder

1 teaspoon ground ginger

½ teaspoon ground cardamom

¼ teaspoon dried *besobela* (page 38) or
    ground Thai basil

⅛ teaspoon ground cinnamon

½ tablespoon sea salt

Remove and discard the stems of the chilies and, if the variety is on the hotter side, shake out the seeds. Grind in an electric spice or coffee grinder and transfer to a mixing bowl.

Heat a small dry frying pan over medium–low heat and separately dry-toast the nigella seeds, cloves, and ajowan for about 2 minutes each, stirring and shaking the pan until aromatic. Transfer the toasted spices to the mixing bowl, add the onion powder, garlic powder, ginger, cardamom, Thai basil, cinnamon, and salt and stir to combine.

Working in batches if needed, grind all the spices together to a fine, even powder. Store in an airtight container in a dry, cool place.

 በርበሬ

Berbere Spice Blend

A good *berbere* powder is hot, but not blisteringly so. That is the job of it's spice cousin *mitmita* (see page 47). *Berbere* is instead zesty, tangy, and pungent. The heat level of the final spice blend is dependent on the specific dried chilies used to make it, and which region the chilies are from. Across Ethiopia chilies vary widely on the scoville scale, so *berbere* can carry any level of heat depending on where it's made. In Ethiopia, the best variety of *berbere* comes from the Mareko chili. These chilies have a curved, smooth texture, with leathery red-maroon skin, and are 3½–6 inches (9–15 cm) long.

Traditionally, several days are needed for the complete preparation of *berbere* powder. The process begins during November, when farmers first harvest and sun-dry the chilies in the Ethiopian heat for about two weeks, before taking them to market to sell.

Each household goes to buy their own supply of chilies. Having collected them, the chilies are spread out on a *kesha* (a mat made of palm leaves) across doorsteps of their homes and sometimes even on their roofs. As the chilies dry, the discolored ones will be removed and the rest will be left on the mat to completely dry until all remaining moisture is gone.

It is now that the real *berbere* preparation can begin. The chilies are transferred to a *doneya* (a wool sack), which is then tapped with a wooden stick or rubbed by hand. The tapping, or rubbing, breaks down the chilies and removes the tiny particles of unbearably hot powder. What remains in the wool sack is then pounded in a traditional mortar called a *muketcha*, before the next stage begins.

The next stage is *ereteb kemem*, which translates to "wet spices," known as the wet aromatic phase. It includes garlic, ginger, rue seeds, *besobela* seeds (Ethiopian basil), and certain fresh herbs. These are pounded and blended to a chunky paste. Next, this paste is mixed with the crushed chilies in a large wooden container called a *gebete*. Some of this mixture is returned to the mortar and pounded once more to get an extra fine texture. The result is a thick red paste called *delez berbere*, the initial form of *berbere*. Next, the *delez* mixture is returned

to the *gebete*, and is pressed flat before being sprinkled with "dry *tej*," the advanced fermented version of Ethiopian honey wine (see page 10). To finish the aromatic wet phase, *besobela* leaves, whose seeds were used earlier, are layered on top of the pressed *deleh*, before the mixture is tightly covered with a *lémat*, a curved woven straw plate.

At this point, the *delez berbere* is left to mature in the *gebete*, in a dry place, for two days. After this it is opened to release an enchanting mixture of sweet, spicy, and fresh aromas. These aromas are characteristic of *berbere* season, and fill the air. Households then re-dry the chili paste in the sun, crumbling it over their *kesha* mats and leaving it to dry again.

The end of November and beginning of December is a magical time for sensory pleasure in Ethiopia. Neighborhoods are covered with crumbled *delez berbere*, which brings a captivating scent to the entire country. Year after year, this unique spicing art imparts a priceless memory on the younger generations, who are ready to embrace, as we did, the prized culinary legacy of their birthright.

The very last phase of making *berbere* is known as the intensification stage, or "dry spices" stage. This consists of lightly toasting dry whole spices such as *korerima* (page 39), ajowan, nigella, long pepper, and more, to awake their dormant aromas. These spices are then mixed with the crumbled and fully dried *delez berbere*, before the whole mixture is sent to flour milling plants to be ground into the famous powder form that we commonly call *berbere*.

Berbere Deleh Paste

*This is the paste form of **berbere**. Moistening the chili-based spice blend and letting it stand mellows its kick and reduces the cooking time needed for the flavors to lose their aggressiveness. Ideally, it is prepared in advance and stored for many days. Yet recipes today often forgo this step and simply use the dry **berbere** spice blend instead. When preparing stews, some cooks make a quick paste as the first step in the recipe and let it mellow slightly as they prepare the **kulet** (onion base), but the older generation and the best cooks always have **berbere deleh** in their kitchens.*

MAKES ABOUT 6 TABLESPOONS (3½ oz/100 g)

¼ teaspoon fenugreek seeds
generous ½ cup (1¾ oz/50 g) *berbere* spice blend (page 40)
1 teaspoon mild vegetable oil

In a saucepan, combine ½ cup (125 ml) of water and the fenugreek seeds and bring to a boil. Immediately remove from the heat and drain, reserving the liquid. Discard the fenugreek.

In a mixing bowl, blend the *berbere* with the oil and, adding a little at a time, about 3½ tablespoons (50 ml) of the reserved liquid to form a thick paste. Add in a touch more liquid if needed. Store in an airtight container in the refrigerator for up to 1 month.

Mekelesha Spice Blend

*Not all of the popular spice blends in Ethiopia are based on chilies, and **mekelesha** uses none at all. Instead, the aromatic spices balance the heat of a dish and the name in fact means "to dilute." As it is intended for use as a finishing spice blend, it is important that it is added only for the last few minutes of cooking so that its many delectable aromatic notes are preserved.*

Use freshly ground cardamom, if possible. Dry-toast the pods in dry frying pan until aromatic, then remove the seeds with your fingers and grind in a mortar and pestle.

MAKES JUST OVER 1 TABLESPOON

2 teaspoons ground cinnamon
½ teaspoon ground cloves
½ teaspoon ground long pepper or black pepper
½ teaspoon freshly ground cardamom

In a small bowl, blend the spices together to a homogeneous mixture. Store in an airtight container in a dry, cool place.

Awaze Dipping Sauce

*This spicy dipping sauce is made from whisking **berbere** spice blend with **tej** (honey wine or mead), wine, beer, the potent, anise-flavored spirit, **arak**, or even just a mixture of water and honey. Culturally, the **berbere** used for **awaze** is slightly different from regular **berbere** since most of the grains must be removed in the making to gain a final strong red color and mellow spicy taste. No matter how it is prepared, the goal is to find a balance between the spicy, sweet, and sour elements, and to revive some of the subtle spices used in preparing **berbere**.*

* **Awaze** generally accompanies meats—it is key with **kurt** (a raw meat dish, see page 147) and used in preparing strips of **zilzil tibs** (see page 130)—but it can also be used with vegetarian dishes such as **dinich alicha** (see page 88) or **ater kik alicha** (page 102). While it should be runny and drizzle off a spoon, the final consistency varies from house to house.*

* There are three versions below; choose your preferred ingredients and follow the relevant method.*

**MAKES ABOUT ⅓ CUP
(3½ oz/100 g)**

Version One
¼ cup (¾ oz/20 g) *berbere* spice blend (page 40)
⅓ cup (80 ml) *tej*

Version Two
¼ teaspoon honey
⅓ cup (80 ml) medium-dry white wine
¼ cup (¾ oz/20 g) *berbere* spice blend (page 40)

Version Three
¼ cup (¾ oz/20 g) *berbere* spice blend (page 40)
⅓ cup (80 ml) pastis, ouzo, or *arake*

For version one, whisk together the *berbere* powder and *tej* in a small bowl until well blended. Store in an airtight container in the refrigerator.

Alternatively, for version two, whisk the honey into the wine in a small bowl until well dissolved. Add the *berbere* powder and whisk again until blended. Store in an airtight container in the refrigerator.

For version three, place the *berbere* powder in a small bowl and whisk with the pastis, ouzo, or *arake* until smooth and it pours easily off a spoon. Add a touch more liquid if needed. Store in an airtight container in the refrigerator.

Mitmita Spice Blend

*Berbere isn't the only popular chili blend used in the Ethiopian kitchen and **mitmita**, its closely related cousin, is an even hotter version. However, **mitmita** is more orange in color than the scarlet **berbere** (in part from the large amount of salt it contains) and, unlike **berbere**, is generally used as a dry dip or seasoning. (Keep that salt quantity in mind when seasoning dishes.) This famous version of **mitmita** comes from the Guragé region to the west of Addis Ababa, where people often also add a local, oregano-like herb called **koseret**. For a very quick substitution, mix powdered bird's-eye chilies with salt and a pinch of dried oregano, thyme, and Thai basil.*

MAKES ABOUT 1¾ oz (50 g)

¾ oz (20 g) dried hot red chilies, such as Thai chilies, or 2 heaped tablespoons ground cayenne pepper

1 tablespoon salt

1½ teaspoons ajowan seeds

1 teaspoon dried *koseret* (page 39) or equal amount dried oregano and thyme

¾ teaspoon nigella seeds

In an electric spice or coffee grinder, grind the chilies with the salt, ajowan seeds, *koseret*, and nigella seeds. Pass it through a sieve and grind again to a fine, homogeneous blend. Store in an airtight container in a dry, cool place.

Niter Kebbeh, the Ethiopian Spiced Clarified Butter

One would expect Ethiopia, with the leading livestock population on the continent,[1] to produce a considerable amount of dairy products, and yet reality is quite the opposite. While various Ethnic groups on the land consume cow milk, camel milk, and goat milk, the overall consumption of dairy remains quite limited and its byproducts are traditionally undiversified. With very few recipes that use buttermilk, like *hazo* (see *tihelo,* page 139), and even less variety of local cheese available throughout the multiple traditions, Ethiopians seem to have overlooked most secondary dairy products, choosing to specialize in butter instead.

With a rich culinary legacy, the art of cooking and scenting butter has flourished in Ethiopia to the point where our cuisine today can easily be identified through the mesmerizing aroma of this key ingredient, diffused from all Ethiopian restaurants worldwide. Commonly called *niter kebbeh*, it translates to "clarified spiced butter" and the process starts by storing whole milk for a minimum of three days in a dry cool place. Then this milk, which has become yogurt, is transferred to an *ensera* and shaken until butter forms. While an *ensera* is traditionally used to transport water, an *ensera* with a stick-hole is on the other hand used only to prepare butter and *ayb* cheese. The hole allows a stick to be inserted to check if the byproduct is ready.

Once the basic butter is extracted, it is usually classified in two groups: *lega* (table butter) and *yebesele* (aged butter). Both are sold in open markets, stored in traditional earthenware or plastic. Here, the fundamental step in the process of traditional butter clarification happens: the addition of water. Adding water to a pot of melted butter is called *mangor*, which means

to clean. *Mangor* enables the separation of any impurity that could be found in butter purchased from open markets. When water is added to the melted butter the pot is taken off the heat, and the mixture is given 24 hours to settle. After just one day, a layer of translucent water is formed under the floating clarified butter. By this point, the water has played another crucial role beyond extracting impurities and whey, which is giving the necessary moisture to the clarified butter. The water is poured off by piercing holes on the surface of the butter and tilting the pot. The pot is then put back on fire for the final, very slow, and captivating, spicing stage of *niter kebbeh* (see page 52).

Many individuals familiar with Ethiopian cuisine would tell you *niter kebbeh* is the central ingredient in the local cuisine accountable for the similar pronounced taste to all our non-fasting recipes (see page 93). But I believe *niter kebbeh* reserves one last secret: specificity. Each region in Ethiopia has preferences in term of aging processes, spicing (as per available spices in the area), and also as to the moment *niter kebbeh* is added to a recipe (see map on page 8). The Garagé region, for instance, focuses on *koseret* and *korerima* as dominant spicing agents in the making of *niter kebbeh*, making it ideal for the preparation of *kitfo* (see page 144). Afar chooses to integrate honey in the making, while Harar prefers using fenugreek, crafting its version for an ideal fit to recipes originating in its region. Highlands prefer aged *niter kebbeh*, bringing an additional flavor to stews like *doro wat* (see page 170) while Gambela avoids spicing the butter, instead enjoying its simple prolonged aged taste. Hence, culturally sensitive cooks say each *niter kebbeh* is aimed to perfectly complement specific dishes of our abundant non-fasting traditional recipes.

---

1. International Trade Administration *Ethiopia—Livestock* (2017). Available at www.export.gov/article?id=Ethiopia-Livestock

Spiced Clarified Butter

Niter kebbeh is the soul of Ethiopian cuisine. Used in almost all non-fasting recipes (see page 93), it brings a unique flavor that anyone who has ever stepped into an Ethiopian kitchen (or restaurant), anywhere in the world, would instantly recognize.

Clarified butter is common in many culinary traditions and made from the simple process of heating butter until the water evaporates and the milk solids separate so that a golden oil can be strained off and stored. In South Asia, the solids are also left to brown a little, which gives the clarified butter or "ghee" a nutty flavor. In Ethiopia, however, cooks take the heating process a step further and simmer a range of spices, even onions and garlic, before filtering, and the result is a fragrant, flavorful oil that brings a distinctive rich texture and aroma to many dishes. Once you've tried it, you'll see that infusing clarified butter is a wonderful technique to have in your repertoire, and you can experiment with all kinds of flavors.

*Authentic **niter kebbeh** uses an aromatic dried herb called **koseret**, and sometimes **besobela**. Oregano and thyme make pretty good substitutions but if you want to capture a stronger, leafy herbiness, substitute the dry herbs for chopped fresh Thai basil and sage. Note, though, that using fresh herbs will turn the normally golden **niter kebbeh** an olive green color. This cooking process of **niter kebbeh** is not strictly the traditional manner in which is it made in Ethiopia, instead it has been revised for western cooking.*

MAKES ABOUT 1¼ CUPS (10½ oz/300 g)

1 lb 2 oz (500 g) unsalted butter
1 teaspoon nigella seeds
½ teaspoon cardamom seeds
1 teaspoon coriander seeds (optional)
1 teaspoon dried *koseret* (page 39) or equal amounts of dried oregano and thyme
1 teaspoon dried *besobela* (page 38) or Thai basil

In a heavy-bottomed saucepan, melt the butter over low heat, skimming off the foam. Cook for about 5 minutes until the solid, milky residue has sunk to the bottom, but do not let the solids darken. Remove the pan from the heat and allow to cool a little, then strain the liquid into a clean saucepan and discard the solids.

Sprinkle the nigella, cardamom, and coriander seeds, if using, into the pan and cook over low heat for 5–10 minutes until aromatic, stirring gently from time to time. Add the *koseret* and *besobela* and continue to cook for 5 minutes, stirring gently. Watch to make sure it does not burn and the oil does not darken.

Remove the pan from the heat and leave to settle for 10 minutes. Strain through a cheesecloth into a clean glass jar. Once completely cool, cover tightly and store in the refrigerator, where it will solidify, for up to two months.

Homemade Ethiopian Brown Mustard

Ethiopian mustard is a bit runnier than its Western counterparts, since it is more of a dip than a spread. It is made from three main types of mustard seeds, from mild to sharp: whitish-yellow, brown, and black (brown being the most common in Ethiopia). The important thing is to leave it for a couple of days in order for the bitterness to fade and the nose-pinching pungency to emerge. It accompanies **kurt** *(raw meat, see page 147) and gives a lovely kick to the chilled lentil salad* **azifa** *(see page 104). However, as it does not contain vinegar, it cannot be kept for as long as standard store-bought mustards. Keep for a maximum of three days in the refrigerator.*

Here, I have provided a nice simplified mustard recipe for the home cook. Traditionally, we use a slightly different method: the freshly ground mustard seeds are mixed with a small amount of boiling water and pressed into a thick paste. This is then rolled into balls about 2 inches (5 cm) in diameter, which are kept submerged in cold water for some days. A pinch of the mustard ball is used to whisk with some hot water and oil as needed.

MAKES ABOUT ½ CUP (125 ml)

5 tablespoons brown mustard seeds
¼ teaspoon salt
2 tablespoons olive oil

Grind the mustard seeds to a powder using an electric spice or coffee grinder. Transfer to a small mixing bowl, add the salt, and moisten with the olive oil. Whisk in about 3 tablespoons of hot water and let stand for a few moments, before whisking in 1 more tablespoon of hot water. It should be saucy but not overly runny.

Spoon into a clean glass jar, tightly cover, and refrigerate before using, ideally for two days. Whisk again before serving.

Store in the refrigerator in a sealed container for up to three days.

Fresh Chili Dipping Sauce

*Daata is a thick, fresh (and tongue-shriveling hot) chili sauce most commonly used as a dip for raw meat and fish. While the country's most renowned chilies come from the area of Alaba, south of Addis Ababa in the Rift Valley, connoisseurs know the best skills in preparing **daata** are in Hawassa, the region's main city. The best batches are still laboriously ground on a stone mortar.*

Much of a chili pepper's searing heat resides in the core and many cooks know that, by removing the seeds and cutting out the veins, you can moderate it somewhat. I often separate the seeds from the chilies before grinding, and then add an amount back into the blend, according to taste. Rue is a herb that is hard to find, but can be substituted with cilantro, which will also bring a touch of freshness to the paste. Taste as you go and add more herbs as desired.

MAKES ABOUT ½ CUP (125 ml)

3½ oz (100 g) fresh hot green or red chilies (such as bird's-eye, serrano, or fresno)

2 tablespoons coarsely chopped fresh *besobela* (page 38) or Thai basil

1 tablespoon finely chopped fresh rosemary

1 tablespoon coarsely chopped fresh rue (page 39) or ½ tablespoon coarsely chopped cilantro

1 tablespoon salt

Wearing rubber gloves, wipe the chilies with a damp cloth. Cut off and discard the stems, then shake the seeds out of the pods into a bowl and reserve. Remove some of the veins if desired.

Using a food processor or a mortar and pestle, grind the chilies, *besobela*, rosemary, rue, and salt. Blend in as many chili seeds as desired, then taste for flavoring and add more fresh herbs if needed.

3

Breakfast

Barley Porridge with Niter Kebbeh and Served with Yogurt

Genfo is a much-beloved breakfast staple across the country, with versions prepared by many of Ethiopia's distinct cultural groups. While traditionally made with barley flour, some blend barley and wheat together or use corn flour or, in the south of the country, enset flour (bula, see page 30). However, it is never made with wheat alone, since it becomes too elastic. This recipe is a version from Oromia and is traditionally served from a communal bowl. To eat, take a spoonful of genfo and dip it into the spicy, melted niter kebbeh in the middle.

If the bottom scorches while cooking, do not scrape and stir it in. Simply avoid the burnt parts when removing from the pan.

As one Ethiopian proverb reminds us, this thick porridge should be eaten as soon as it is prepared: "Porridge and love should be served hot, if cold, they will lose a lot."

SERVES 4

¼ teaspoon salt

1¾ cups (9 oz/250 g) barley flour or an even blend of barley and wheat flours

⅔ cup (5½ oz/150 g) *niter kebbeh* (page 52) or clarified butter, or more to taste

1 tablespoon *berbere* spice blend (page 40), or more to taste

plain whole-milk yogurt, to serve

In a large non-stick saucepan, bring 2 cups (500 ml) of water to a boil and add the salt. In a separate saucepan, bring another 2 cups (500 ml) of water to a boil and keep hot.

Sift the flour into the first saucepan and stir well. As the mixture thickens, gradually work in the boiling water from the other pan, stirring continuously with a stout wooden spoon for about 5 minutes (there might be some water left over). The *genfo* should be a thick but springy dough with a slightly roasted aroma. Do not let the bottom scorch.

Place the dough in a large, round serving bowl. Using your hands or a large spoon, shape it into a ball and form a well in the top.

In a small saucepan, melt the *niter kebbeh* over low heat and stir in the *berbere*, then pour into the well.

Spoon yogurt around the side of the *genfo*. Take a spoonful of the *niter kebbeh* from the well and drizzle it over the yogurt. Serve with spoons and eat directly from the serving bowl.

Layered Flatbread Pastries with Honey

*This simple pastry with honey makes a typical breakfast in Harar and Dire Dawa, in the east of the country, where it is often pan-fried and sold at small stalls as street food. It can also be found in restaurants and hotels as a classic breakfast option. The perfect **fetira** has leaves of pastry, which are made by folding the dough over itself. Large bubbles should form on the surface of the pastry during cooking.*

In a large mixing bowl, sift in the flour. Add the salt and oil and, with your hands, begin working in about 1 cup (240 ml) of warm water. Mix well without overworking the dough. Transfer to a clean surface and lightly knead until elastic, about 5 minutes.

Divide the dough into six even pieces and form into balls about 2 inches (5 cm) in diameter—about the size of large plums. Place on a plate, lightly brush with oil, and cover with a damp cloth or plastic wrap. Set aside to rest for 10–15 minutes.

Oil a rolling pin. Working on a lightly oiled surface and with one piece of dough at a time, roll out each ball into a squareish sheet, stretched as thinly as possible without breaking the dough. Brush the sheet with oil and carefully fold the top and bottom thirds inwards to make a rectangle. Then fold the outer two thirds inwards again, lightly brushing each of the folds with oil, until you have a 4–6 inch (10–15 cm) square. Roll again to flatten the square to around ¼ inch (5 mm) thick.

MAKES 6 PASTRIES

3¼ cups (14 oz/400 g) all-purpose flour

1 teaspoon salt

3 tablespoons sunflower, canola, or other mild
   vegetable oil, plus extra for oiling

clear honey, to serve

Heat a heavy, dry frying pan or griddle over a medium–high heat. Gently lay the pastry on the hot surface and cook for about 5 minutes until golden, flipping from time to time. When the dough begins to puff up a bit, brush the sides with oil to get a golden, crispy texture. Transfer to a platter and keep warm.

Roll out, fold, and cook the remaining pastries. Cut each in half diagonally and serve warm with honey drizzled generously over the top.

Flatbread Pastries Stuffed with Egg

These delightful, egg-stuffed pastries are served in bite-size pieces. While this recipe cooks them in a dry pan, they can also be shallow-fried in oil. If cooking them this way, lift them out of the oil with a slotted spoon and drain well on paper towels before serving.

MAKES 6 STUFFED PASTRIES

3¼ cups (14 oz/400 g) all-purpose flour

1 teaspoon salt, plus more for seasoning

3 tablespoons sunflower, canola, or other mild vegetable oil, plus more for brushing the dough

3 large eggs

⅓ cup (1¾ oz/50 g) finely chopped yellow onion

¼ cup (1½ oz/40 g) finely chopped jalapeño or green pepper

Sift the flour into a large mixing bowl. Add the salt and oil and, with your hands, begin working in about 1 cup (240 ml) of warm water. Mix well without overworking the dough. Transfer to a clean surface and lightly knead until elastic, about 5 minutes.

Divide the dough into six even pieces and form into balls about 2 inches (5 cm) in diameter—about the size of large plums. Place on a plate, lightly brush with oil, and cover with a damp cloth or plastic wrap. Set aside to rest for 10–15 minutes.

In a bowl, whisk the eggs. Stir in the onion and jalapeño and season with salt—you should have about 1 cup (240 ml) of filling.

Oil a rolling pin. Working on a lightly oiled surface and with one piece of dough at a time, roll out each ball into a thin, squareish sheet 8–10 inches (20–25 cm) in diameter (the final size is not too important since the pastries will be cut before serving). If rolling with oil is too challenging, dust some wheat flour on the surface instead. Traditional cooks flatten the dough by hand, tapping it against a marble surface to flatten it without breaking.

Heat a dry heavy wok over medium heat. Gently lay the dough in the middle of the pan and add the egg mixture. Fold the four sides of the dough over the eggs. Immediately add 1–2 tablespoons of oil to the pan and cook for 5 minutes, flipping a few times and each time brushing the pastry with a little oil, until golden and crispy. Set aside and keep warm.

Roll out, fill, and cook the remaining pastries. Chop into 1 inch (2.5 cm) pieces and serve warm.

Breakfast Fava Beans

Ful medames—mashed brown fava beans—might be the national dish of Egypt and a favorite in parts of the Middle East, but it is also hugely popular for breakfast in Ethiopia. And whereas those other versions often come garnished with olive oil, parsley, lemon, garlic, or even tahini, in Ethiopia it gets mashed into onions, topped with scrambled eggs, adorned with yogurt, sliced onions, and a scattering of chopped jalapeños.

*Look for cans of beans that read **foul medames** (or a spelling thereabouts) in Middle Eastern grocery stores. Alternatively, the recipe can also be made with dried fava beans, but be sure to use the small brown ones rather than the larger dried green ones with much thicker skins. Soak overnight and then boil until tender. While cooking times vary depending on the quality and the age of the beans, expect 2–2 ½ hours at a gentle simmer in unsalted water.*

*The dish is excellent with the layered fruit drink **spris** (see page 213) or a glass of spiced tea, **kimem chai**. Serve with crusty white bread and, to heighten the flavors, add a spoonful of tomato paste to the cooking onions.*

SERVES 2

14 oz (400 g) can cooked small brown
    fava beans (*foul medames*)
1 medium yellow onion
3 tablespoons sunflower, canola, or other
    mild vegetable oil
salt
1 ripe plum tomato, cored and finely chopped
2 eggs, whisked
½ medium jalapeño pepper, sliced, to garnish
plain yogurt, to serve

Place the beans in a saucepan with about 2 cups (500 ml) of water. Bring to a boil, then remove from the heat and leave them in the liquid until ready to use.

Finely chop about three-quarters of the onion. Thinly slice the remaining quarter and set aside for garnishing.

Place a large sauté pan over medium–low heat, add 2 tablespoons of the oil and the chopped onion, and cook for 8–10 minutes until soft and translucent. Using a slotted spoon, transfer the beans to the sauté pan, season with salt, and add a touch of the cooking liquid. Mash with a ladle or the back of a serving spoon and stir well to blend everything together. Tip in more liquid if needed so that the mixture is moist. Transfer to a serving bowl. Place the sliced raw onion on one side of the beans and the tomato on the other.

In a frying pan, heat the remaining tablespoon of oil and scramble the eggs with a pinch of salt. When cooked, tip the eggs over the beans and scatter the jalapeño over the top. Serve with yogurt in a bowl on the side.

Butter-Soaked Flatbread

*There are a number of dishes made across the country that are akin to large, thin "pancakes" that are torn into pieces and seasoned with **niter kebbeh** and some spices. This one, from Oromia region, is popular for breakfast and provides a lovely balance of sweet and savory flavors. Note: It is important to tear or cut the **chechebsa** into pieces and blend with the butter while still warm, since this allows the flavors to penetrate the dough and to keep the moisture from escaping and drying out the dough.*

SERVES 2–3

generous 1 cup (5 oz/140 g) all-purpose flour

salt

oil, for greasing the pan

3½ tablespoons (1¼ oz/50 g) *niter kebbeh* (page 52) or clarified butter

½ tablespoon *berbere* spice blend (page 40)

plain yogurt, to serve

clear honey, to serve

In a large mixing bowl, combine the flour with a generous pinch of salt and whisk in about 1 cup (240 ml) of water until you have a thin pancake-like batter.

Heat a large griddle or 12–14 inch (30–35 cm) frying pan over medium heat and very lightly grease with oil. Working in batches, ladle the batter into the pan, tilting it a little to thinly coat the base. Cook for 2–3 minutes until golden, then flip, cover with a lid, and cook for a further 2 minutes, or until this side is golden and the pancake is no longer doughy on the inside. Transfer to a plate and cover to keep warm. Repeat with the remaining batter.

Meanwhile, in a small saucepan, melt the *niter kebbeh* and stir in the *berbere*.

When the pancakes are still warm but cool enough to handle, cut them into pieces and place in a serving bowl.

Pour the melted *niter kebbeh* over the *chechebesa* in the bowl and turn the pieces over until well coated. Serve warm with yogurt and honey on the side, to add as desired.

Torn Injera with Flaxseed Dressing

*Most cooked Ethiopian dishes are served warm and yet this one is a rare exception. It is served cold, often as part of a fasting spread (see page 93), and provides a lovely cool balance alongside spicy legume stews and vegetable dishes (see page 77). **Injera** often gets torn and pushed into the sauce, but a more elegant presentation is to cut it into strips and roll it before gently pushing it into the liquid.*

There are two kinds of flaxseed: golden and reddish-brown. The latter is more common in Ethiopia, but you can use either.

SERVES 2–4

generous ½ cup (3½ oz/100 g) brown or
    golden flaxseed

salt

1 medium yellow onion, finely chopped

2 ripe medium plum tomatoes, peeled, seeded,
    and finely chopped

½ medium jalapeño pepper, seeded and
    chopped, to garnish

injera (page 20)

Heat a small dry frying pan over medium–low heat. Add the flaxseed and lightly dry-toast for about 2 minutes, stirring and shaking the pan, until aromatic. Transfer to a dish and leave to cool. Once cool, grind using an electric spice or coffee grinder.

In a large bowl, mix the flaxseed with 2 cups (480 ml) of cold water and blend to a light, runny paste. Generously season with salt, then stir in the onion, tomatoes, and jalapeño. Add a touch more water if needed to keep the mixture loose. Roll the *injera* and cut it into strips ¾ inch (2 cm) wide. Gently push into the liquid to allow the *injera* to soak up the sauce. Transfer to a clean bowl, chill in the fridge, and serve cold.

Simple Fasting Bulgur

Bulgur—wheat that has been parboiled, dried, and then cracked—makes a popular breakfast dish in Ethiopia when cooked with spiced clarified butter and served with scrambled eggs. This is the fasting version (see page 93)—without clarified butter—and is often served with firfir (pieces of torn injera in sauce, see pages 136 and 185). Filling, simple to prepare, and subtle in taste, it also offers a contrast in texture to a number of dishes. Serve with Dirkosh Injera Firfir (page 136) and/or Yehabesha Enkulal Firfir (page 185).

SERVES 2–4

3 tablespoons sunflower, canola, or other mild vegetable oil

½ medium red or yellow onion, finely chopped

1¼ cups (6 oz/175 g) bulgur

2½ cups (600 ml) vegetable stock

salt

Place a large sauté pan over medium–low heat, add the oil and onion, and cook for about 5 minutes until soft. Add the bulgur and cook, stirring continuously, for about 2 minutes until semi-translucent and aromatic.

Pour in the stock, season with salt, and stir well. Cover and simmer for about 12 minutes until the bulgur is tender and the liquid absorbed. Add in a little more stock (or water) if needed. Fluff with a fork and serve.

Whole Dried Peas with Cut Injera

Fitfit *essentially consists of shredded (or cut up)* **injera***, which is pushed down into a flavorful, onion-based sauce.* **Firfir** *is similar but has a little* **berbere** *in it too.*

*   This dish uses whole—rather than split—dried peas. Whereas split peas tend to disintegrate, these remain whole and keep their shape. The dried peas sold locally in Ethiopia tend to be yellow rather than green.*

SERVES 6

1¼ cups (9 oz/250 g) whole dried yellow peas

3 tablespoons sunflower, canola, or other mild vegetable oil

1 medium red or yellow onion, finely chopped

1 teaspoon finely chopped garlic

½ teaspoon grated or finely chopped fresh ginger

¼ teaspoon ground turmeric

¼ teaspoon ground ajowan

salt

2–3 jalapeño peppers, split and seeded, to garnish (optional)

injera (page 20)

Place the peas in a large bowl and pick over and discard any debris. Soak in cold water overnight, then drain, rinse, and drain again.

Place the peas in a saucepan, cover with cold water, and bring to a boil. Cover the pot, reduce the heat, and cook at a low boil for about 30 minutes until tender. Strain, reserving the liquid.

Place a large sauté pan or wide saucepan over medium–low heat, add the oil and onion, and cook for 8–10 minutes until soft and translucent. Stir in the garlic and ginger and cook for a minute until aromatic. Stir in the turmeric and ajowan, cover, and cook over low heat for 10 minutes. Add a touch of water if needed to keep it from scorching.

Add the reserved peas, season with salt, and stir to blend well. Pour in about 1½ cups (350 ml) of the reserved liquid and stir well again. Cover and cook over low heat for about 10 minutes until the stew thickens a little but is still saucy and slightly runny. Transfer to a serving bowl. Garnish with the jalapeños, if desired.

Roll the *injera* and cut into strips 1 inch (2.5 cm) wide. Arrange the *injera* rolls along the edges of the serving bowl and gently push part-way down into the sauce. Serve immediately.

Spicy Tomato Stew

In Ethiopia most men are not accustomed to cooking for themselves, except perhaps for this simple dish or the famous Daka Wot of Lalibela, made by men only. Considering Sils is prepared by many almost everyday, multiple versions of this very simple and popular breakfast exist. However, this is the most popular version: stewy and with a slightly chunky body.

SERVES 4–6

1 lb 2 oz (500 g) ripe tomatoes, peeled, cored, and seeded

3 tablespoons sunflower, canola, or other mild vegetable oil

2 medium red or yellow onions (about 10½ oz/300 g), finely chopped

1 tablespoon *berbere* spice blend (page 40), or more to taste

salt

injera (page 20), to serve (optional)

Cut the tomatoes into chunky pieces, place in a food processor, and purée.

In a sauté pan, heat the oil over medium–high heat, add the onions, and cook for 2 minutes. Add the *berbere* and cook for 3 minutes, stirring very frequently. Add the tomatoes, season with salt, and cook for 15–20 minutes, until they begin to thicken and have lost about half their moisture but are still a little stewy. Simply enjoy on its own or serve with *injera* or scrambled egg, if you like.

Flaxseed and Banana Purée

This is a healthy breakfast made by my mom and a favorite in my family home.
The purée should be thick and you can use either brown or golden flaxseed, but always
dry-toast it before grinding, since this brings out the sweet, nutty flavors. Serve with a
bowl of seasonal fresh fruit.

SERVES 2

2 tablespoons brown or golden flaxseed
2 ripe bananas, cut into pieces
¼ cup (60 ml) skim milk
seasonal fresh fruit, to serve

Heat a small dry frying pan over medium–low heat. Add the flaxseed and lightly dry-toast for about 2 minutes until aromatic, stirring and shaking the pan. Transfer to a dish to cool. When cool, grind using an electric spice or coffee grinder.

Place the ground flaxseed in a blender or food processor, add the bananas and milk, and blend to a thick, smooth purée. Add a touch more milk if needed. Spoon into small bowls and serve with fresh fruit.

4

Vegetables & Fresh Cheese

Braised Beet Batons with Jalapeño Peppers

The sweet, earthy taste—and vibrant scarlet color—of this beet dish makes a perfect addition to any **beyayenetu** *platter, with its array of spicy dishes (pictured right). The beets also pair perfectly with grilled meat dishes, such as* **siga tibs** *(see page 131).*

When buying fresh beets, look for firm ones with smooth skins that are sold in bunches with their stalks still attached. Be careful when peeling and chopping, since the juice will stain. Although usually served cold, this dish can also be presented warm if desired.

SERVES 4

1 lb (450 g) medium beets

3 tablespoons sunflower, canola, or other mild vegetable oil

1 medium red or yellow onion, finely chopped

2 garlic cloves, finely chopped

salt

½ lemon

jalapeño peppers, seeded and thinly sliced, to garnish

Rinse the beets under running water and peel. Cut in half lengthways and slice into ½ inch (1.5 cm) thick batons, like thick-cut French fries.

Place a large sauté pan or wide saucepan over medium–low heat, add the oil and onion, and cook for 8–10 minutes until soft and translucent. Stir in the garlic and cook for about 1 minute until aromatic.

Add the beets, season with salt, and pour in 1½ cups (350 ml) water. Cover the pan and simmer for 45–60 minutes until fork-tender and the liquid has been absorbed. Add more water if needed or remove the lid to cook off excess liquid towards the end of cooking—the mixture should be moist but not too liquidy.

Transfer to a bowl and leave to cool, then cover with plastic wrap and refrigerate. Before serving, squeeze over the lemon, toss, garnish with jalapeños, and serve chilled.

Homemade Fresh Cheese

A frequent side dish, this fresh cheese refreshes the palate and counterbalances the bold flavors of spicy stews. This quick version is easy to prepare and the final texture is similar to homemade fresh ricotta. Lemon juice causes the milky-white curds to separate from the watery, yellowish whey and the best way to strain it is to line a large colander with cheesecloth or paper towels. However, avoid using UHT (ultra high-temperature) milk that has been heated to above 275°F (135°C) since the curds will not cling together as easily.

*Traditionally, **ayib** is made in Ensera by shaking then cooking the remaining yogurt left from making butter (see page 48). This gives a hint of astringency. Moistening the curds with a little onion juice at the end creates the same effect. Add if you like.*

MAKES 1 LB 2 OZ (500 G)

8½ cups (2 liters) fresh whole milk
½ cup (125 ml) fresh lemon juice
1 medium red onion (optional)

In a heavy-bottomed saucepan, bring the milk to a slow simmer. It should be foamy and steamy and read 185°F (85°C) on a candy thermometer. Do not let it boil. Slowly pour in the lemon juice and stir for a few seconds, then remove from the heat. Allow to stand undisturbed for about 15 minutes until curds form.

Meanwhile, in a food processor, purée the onion, if using. Place the onion purée in a sieve set over a bowl and let it drain, reserving the liquid. Discard the solids.

Moisten a cheesecloth with water, wring it out, and use it to line a large colander. Gently ladle or pour the curds and liquid through the colander, then set aside to drain for 20–60 minutes until the curds have reached their desired level of dryness. Transfer to a bowl. If using, spoon the onion liquid over it.

Store in a sealed container in the refrigerator for up to three days.

Potatoes and Cabbage in Ginger Turmeric Sauce

Atakilt simply means "vegetable" and, with so many fasting days throughout the year (see page 93), our community eats a lot of cooked vegetables. One or two of the potato, cabbage, and carrot combinations that follow are standard in a selection of dishes for a fasting meal.

SERVES 4

½ large head green cabbage (about 1 lb/450 g)

salt

3 tablespoons sunflower, canola, or other mild vegetable oil

2 medium red or yellow onions, thinly sliced

1 tablespoon finely chopped garlic

1 tablespoon grated or finely chopped ginger

½ teaspoon ground turmeric

freshly ground black pepper

2 medium white potatoes, peeled and quartered lengthways

Core the cabbage and cut into 1½ inch (4 cm) square pieces. Place in a large bowl of warm salted water, swish the leaves around to wash thoroughly, and then drain.

Place a large sauté pan or wide saucepan over medium–low heat, add the oil and onions, and cook for about 10 minutes until soft and translucent. Stir in the garlic and ginger and cook for about 1 minute until aromatic. Add the turmeric and season with salt and black pepper.

Work in the cabbage, stirring from the bottom to blend well. Cover the pan and cook for 5 minutes. Add the potatoes and cook for 2 minutes, gently stirring from time to time. Add ¾ cup (175 ml) of hot water, cover, and cook for about 20 minutes until the potatoes are tender. Add a touch more water if needed or remove the lid to cook off any excess liquid towards the end of cooking. The mixture should be moist but not too liquidy. Serve.

Collard Greens with Onions and Fresh Ginger

*This popular vegetarian dish is frequently part of a **tsom beyayenetu**, or fasting platter, on fasting days (see page 93). However, during non-fasting season, it pairs perfectly with **ayib** (fresh cheese, see page 78) or **kitfo** (raw minced meat, see page 144). In Ethiopia, flat-leaf **gomen** is closest to collard greens, a close relative of kale. If using kale rather than collards, the dish will require a little additional water and slightly more cooking time. While collard greens wilt, kale retains its shape better. Also note, traditionally all vegetables are cooked covered with a lid which tends to affect the color of the greens.*

SERVES 4

1 lb 2 oz (500 g) collard greens or kale

2 tablespoons sunflower, canola, or other mild vegetable oil

2 medium red or yellow onions (about 9 oz/ 250 g), finely chopped

3 garlic cloves, finely chopped

2 tablespoons grated or finely chopped ginger

salt

Wash the greens in various changes of cold water. Trim the fibrous stems and, if desired, the tough center vein. Cut the leaves crossways into strips 1 inch (2.5 cm) wide. There should be about 9 oz (250 g) of washed greens.

Place a large sauté pan or wide saucepan over medium–low heat, add the oil and onions, and cook for about 10 minutes until soft and translucent. Stir in the garlic and ginger and cook for about 1 minute until aromatic.

Begin working in the greens, stirring from the bottom upwards to blend well. Season with salt, then tightly cover the pan and cook for 20–30 minutes until tender. Add a touch of water if needed to keep it from scorching. Serve.

Collard Greens with Spiced Butter and Mitmita

This simple dish is one of the staples in the Guragé region, especially during the winter. The cooked greens are finely chopped and mixed with **niter kebbeh** and **mitmita** spice blend (see page 47) and therefore, in many respects, it mimics the dish often served alongside: **kitfo** (see page 144). However, in the Guragé countryside, at my uncle's for instance, it's commonly served with **kocho**, the popular fermented "bread" made from **enset** (page 30).

Kale, now considered a superfood for its high levels of vitamins, minerals, and antioxidants, is a perfect substitute for collard greens here. Look for crisp, dark green leaves and avoid any with ribs that are either dry or wilted enough to bend. Note that kale takes a bit longer to cook than collard greens.

SERVES 2–4

2¼ lb (1 kg) collard greens or kale
salt
3½ tablespoons *niter kebbeh* (page 52) or
    clarified butter, or more to taste
mitmita spice blend (page 47)

Wash the greens in various changes of cold water. Trim the fibrous stems and, if desired, the tough center vein. Cut the leaves crossways into wide strips. There should be about 1 lb 2 oz (500 g) of washed greens.

Bring a large saucepan of water to a boil, add the greens, and boil for 10–15 minutes until tender (kale may take a bit longer).

Drain the greens in a colander and use a ladle or the back of a serving spoon to press out the moisture. Transfer to a chopping board and, while still hot, mince using a large kitchen knife. Wrap in paper towels and press out as much of the moisture as possible.

Place the greens in a frying pan over low heat and season with salt. Stir in the *niter kebbeh* and *mitmita* to taste and toss thoroughly to combine. Serve.

Vegetable Salad

*The French call it **macédoine** and the Spanish **ensaladilla rusa**: a salad of diced cooked vegetables tossed in mayonnaise. This version uses a dressing prepared from **Seljo**, a mix of soy flour and the liquid from soaking crushed sunflower seeds. In Ethiopia, safflower rather than sunflower seeds are used, which are a favorite to crush and soak for a cooking liquid, or even as a drink.*

SERVES 6

1½ cups (4½ oz/125 g) unsalted sunflower seeds in their shells

⅔ cup (2¾ oz/75 g) soy flour

1 tablespoon hot mustard, preferably homemade Ethiopian brown mustard (page 54), or more to taste

1 tablespoon Dijon mustard, or more to taste

salt and freshly ground black pepper

7 oz (200 g) carrots (3 large), diced into ½ inch (1 cm) pieces

7 oz (200 g) green beans, ends trimmed and cut into ½ inch (1 cm) pieces

7 oz (200 g) sweet potatoes (1 large), diced into ½ inch (1 cm) pieces

1½ cups (7 oz/200 g) fresh or frozen peas

6 large lettuce leaves

Bring a saucepan of water to a boil, add the sunflower seeds, and boil for 2–3 minutes to soften. Drain and transfer the seeds to a blender. Pour in 4 cups (950 ml) of water and roughly grind. Transfer to a bowl and leave to soak for 10 minutes. Strain, reserving the liquid and discarding the solids.

In a large saucepan, heat 3 cups (700 ml) of the reserved liquid over medium heat. Gradually whisk in the soy flour, bring to a gentle boil, and cook for about 20 minutes until you have a runny, creamy paste that easily coats the back of a spoon and has lost its raw taste. Remove from the heat and stir in the mustards. Add a little more of the reserved liquid if necessary to keep the mixture saucy—you should have 1¼–1½ cups (300–350 ml). Set aside.

In a pan of lightly salted water, boil the carrots and green beans for about 12 minutes until tender. In another pan, boil the potatoes for about 8 minutes until tender, and in a third, boil the peas for 2–4 minutes until tender. As the vegetables cook, transfer them with a slotted spoon to a bowl of cold water to cool. Drain and set aside.

In a mixing bowl, gently toss the vegetables in the sauce, ensuring everything is thoroughly coated, and season with salt and black pepper.

To serve, divide the lettuce leaves between plates and top each with the salad.

Whole-Grain Teff Salad

While Ethiopia's staple grain, teff (see page 16), is generally milled into flour and used for
injera *(see page 20), the tiny seeds can be cooked and eaten like whole grains. However,
don't overcook them—they should be just tender and retain a little bite.*

SERVES 4–6

9 oz (250 g) *ayib* (fresh cheese, page 78)
   or ricotta

mitmita spice blend (page 47)

1 ¼ cups (9 oz/250 g) whole-grain teff

½ tablespoon finely chopped fresh mint

½ tablespoon finely chopped fresh flat-leaf
   parsley

salt and freshly ground black pepper

mixed lettuce leaves, shredded

cherry tomatoes, cut in half, to garnish

For the vinaigrette

½ cup (125 ml) olive oil

1 tablespoon white wine or balsamic vinegar

½ tablespoon freshly squeezed lemon juice

white pepper

Prepare the fresh cheese, following the instructions on page 78 and adding a pinch of *mitmita* to the milk. Or simply season fresh cheese with *mitmita*.

Heat a large sauté pan over medium heat, add the teff, and dry-toast for 2–3 minutes. Pour in 3 cups (720 ml) of water, cover, and cook for 7–10 minutes, stirring frequently, until the grains are soft but still retain a slight bite. Uncover towards the end if necessary—the grains should be moist but not soggy.

Transfer the teff to a mixing bowl and set aside to cool. Fluff with a fork, add the mint and parsley, season with salt and black pepper, and toss together to combine.

In a small bowl, whisk together the vinaigrette ingredients or shake everything together in a jar. Toss the lettuce leaves and tomatoes with at least three-quarters of the dressing and moisten the teff grains with the remainder.

Divide the salad between individual plates and spoon the teff and fresh cheese into the middle. Serve.

Potatoes and Carrots in Onion Turmeric Sauce

*Dinich Alicha is one of the few potato recipes in the Ethiopian culture, but is definitely one option commonly available on fasting platters (see page 93). Cooking softly with a slightly runny sauce, this dish is a pleasant addition, especially when consumed with **shiro** (see page 103) and **Senig** (see page 97).*

SERVES 4–6

5 tablespoons sunflower, canola, or other mild vegetable oil

4 medium red or yellow onions, finely chopped (about 1 lb 2 oz/500 g)

5 garlic cloves, finely chopped

1 teaspoon ground turmeric

4 medium carrots, peeled and cut into ¼ inch (5 mm) thick rounds

salt

2¼ lb (1 kg) medium white potatoes, peeled and quartered lengthways

1 jalapeño pepper, seeded and sliced

Place a large sauté pan or wide saucepan over medium heat, add the oil and onions, and cook for 10–15 minutes until soft and translucent. Add the garlic and cook for about 1 minute until aromatic. Stir in the turmeric and carrots, then season with salt. Reduce the heat to low, cover, and cook for 5 minutes.

Add the potatoes, stir to mix, and cook for 2 minutes. Cover with 1 cup (250 ml) of hot water and bring to a simmer. Reduce the heat to low, cover, and cook for 15–20 minutes until the potatoes and carrots are tender. Add more water if needed or remove the lid to cook off excess liquid towards the end of cooking—the mixture should be moist but not too liquidy. Add the jalapeño, cook for a final 1–2 minutes, and serve.

ፎሰልያ | FOSELIA

Sautéed String Beans and Carrots

This vegetable dish is a firm favorite since the beans are steamed in their own juices rather than boiled, which heightens their flavor and gives them a lovely final texture. The stewed tomatoes and carrots bring a lovely complimentary sweetness.

SERVES 4

5 tablespoons sunflower, canola, or other
   mild vegetable oil

2 medium red or yellow onions, finely chopped
   (about 9 oz/250 g)

2 garlic cloves, finely chopped

2 ripe plum tomatoes, finely chopped

½ teaspoon ground turmeric

salt

2 carrots, scrubbed

1 lb 2 oz (500 g) string beans, ends trimmed

Place a medium frying pan over medium–low heat. Add 3 tablespoons of the oil and cook the onions for about 10 minutes until soft and translucent. Add the garlic, tomatoes, and turmeric, season with salt, reduce the heat to low, and cook, stirring frequently, for 15 minutes or until the mixture becomes soft and mushy. Add a touch of water if needed to keep it from scorching.

Meanwhile, slice the carrots crossways into thirds and then cut each segment lengthways into eighths so that there are 24 pieces.

In a large sauté pan or wide saucepan over medium–low heat, add the remaining 2 tablespoons of oil and the carrots and beans. Cover snugly with a lid and cook, stirring from time to time, for 25–30 minutes until tender.

Spoon the tomato sauce over the vegetables, toss well, and serve.

Tomato Salad

*This simple tasty salad is very similar in composition to what one can find in Italian cuisine. While the tradition may have been adopted during Italy's presence in Ethiopia during the mid 1930s or originated before that time, the name, **kurt**, refers to the popular dish of cubed raw meat. Indeed, the size, rawness, and even color of the tomatoes makes it look very similar.*

*While often prepared with white vinegar and sunflower oil, using higher-quality vinegar and oil enhances the flavor of the vinaigrette. Some people add **berbere** spice blend (see page 40) to the salad rather than jalapeños, but I find that the fresh and spicy crunch of the peppers is a very pleasing part of the dish.*

SERVES 4–6

¼ cup (60 ml) extra virgin olive oil

1 tablespoon balsamic vinegar

1 tablespoon fresh lemon juice

salt and freshly ground black pepper

1 medium yellow onion, cut into bite-size pieces

4 ripe plum tomatoes, cut into bite-size pieces

1 jalapeño or ½ green pepper, cut into bite-size pieces

In a small bowl, whisk together the oil, vinegar, and lemon juice and season with salt and black pepper (or shake these ingredients together in a jar).

In a large mixing bowl, place the onion, tomatoes, and jalapeño, pour over the vinaigrette, and toss to combine. Cover with plastic wrap and chill until ready to serve. Toss again before serving.

Hidden Monasteries and EOC

Christianity

Fishermen glide among the shallows of Lake Tana to toss nets for tilapia and Nile perch from *tankwa*, low-riding canoe-like pirogues made out of papyrus material, that look strikingly similar to those narrow boats of early Egypt.[1]

Round in shape and some 30 miles across, the lake is the country's largest. It is also the source of the Blue Nile, or Abay Wenz, "great river." After dropping over the thunderous Tis Isat Falls ("smoke of fire"),[2] the river begins its sweeping thousand-mile course to join the White Nile in Khartoum, Sudan, linking Ethiopia with the ancient world downstream.

There are thirty-some islands on the lake, many of which are home to Ethiopian Orthodox Christian monasteries. From the late thirteenth until the early seventeenth century, when Gondar was established as the capital, the shores of Lake Tana were the center of the Christian Empire,[3] and a number of the monasteries date from this period.

The Orthodox Christian Church in Ethiopia predates even Tana's oldest monasteries by nearly a full millennium, though. In the early fourth century AD, the Aksumite king, Ezana II, converted to Christianity around 320 AD and adapted it as the state religion. And, apart from a decade in the seventeenth century when the ruler briefly embraced Catholicism, it has remained so. (Part of the Coptic Orthodox Church of Alexandria until 1959, it then became the independent Ethiopian Orthodox Tewahedo Church.)

No other single event in Ethiopia's long history is remotely comparable in lasting influence, except perhaps Judaism, which was embraced by Menelik I, son of Makeda Queen of Sheba. It is said Hebrew and Sabean had influences on Geez, an offspring of the south Semitic language used in the Ethiopian Orthodox Tewahedo Church. Geez is the antecedent of all Semitic languages spoken today in Ethiopia, including Amharic, with its 33 basic characters. Successive rulers have based matters of state, society, and culture upon Christianity.[4]

It has strongly shaped almost all art and architecture ventures: the magnificent rock-hewn churches in Lalibela are unrivaled monuments to the faith, and one of nine World Heritage Sites found in the country. The intricate silver Coptic crosses are among the finest jewelry ever tooled, and the narrative frescoes that cover walls and ceilings of churches and monasteries across the country are without artistic equal in the country.

Fasting

But the religion also had an incomparable impact on our cuisine. Dietary restrictions that require abstaining from all meat, eggs, and dairy for half of the year have keenly shaped Ethiopians' daily diet. There are about 250 fasting days a year, 180 of which are obligatory for all Orthodox Christians[5]; the rest are for priests, monks, nuns, and other special groups within the church. Wednesdays and Fridays are always fasting days—the former in remembrance of the betrayal of Christ, the latter in remembrance of his crucifixion and death. And there is a series of lengthy periods throughout the year, including 40 days for Advent before Christmas and 56 days for Lent before Easter. On fasting days, the observants do not eat until 3pm.

The fasting periods are taken seriously in Ethiopia. And so are the great feasts that follow. Fasting meals are vegan (a concept developed long before the term vegan was even coined, in 1944),[6] with legumes and vegetables forming their core. While the dishes that top a *tsom beyaynetu* (fasting platter) do not have spiced clarified butter (*niter kebbeh*), they are rarely bland and often quite spicy.

1. Philip Briggs, *Ethiopia* (Bradt Travel Guides), p.189.
2. "The Blue Nile" *National Geographic* (2000).
3. Philip Briggs, *Ethiopia* (Bradt Travel Guides), p.215.
4. "Upon Christianity Ethiopia based its state, society, and culture."
5. George Gerster, *Churches in Rock*, (Phaidon), p.49.
6. www.merriam-webster.com/dictionary/vegan

Spicy Pumpkin Stew

*While shopping in weekly souqs or outdoor markets around Addis Ababa, one common item for sale all around the country is **duba** (pumpkin). Smallhold farmers generally intercrop **duba** with maize or other perennial crops, and bring them to the souq, where they sell them cut into large pieces. The amounts here serve a number of people as part of a spread of vegetable dishes. This also makes an excellent side dish to accompany chicken, fish, or meat.*

SERVES 2–4

3 tablespoons sunflower, canola, or other mild
   vegetable oil

2 medium red or yellow onions, finely chopped
   (about 9 oz/250 g)

2 garlic cloves, finely chopped

1 tablespoon *berbere* spice blend (page 40),
   or more to taste

¼ teaspoon ground cardamom

1 lb 2 oz (500 g) peeled and seeded pumpkin,
   butternut squash, or acorn squash, cut into
   1 inch (2.5 cm) cubes

salt

In a large Dutch oven or sauté pan, heat the oil over medium–low heat, add the onions, and cook for about 10 minutes until soft and translucent. Stir in the garlic, *berbere*, and cardamom, reduce the heat to low, cover, and cook for 10 minutes, stirring frequently. Add a touch of water if needed to keep it from scorching.

Add the pumpkin, season with salt, and cover with 1 cup (250 ml) of water. Partly cover the pan and cook over medium–low heat for 25–35 minutes until the pumpkin is fork-tender. Gently stir from time to time to keep from sticking, but avoid mashing the pumpkin as it softens. Add more water if needed or remove the lid to cook off excess liquid towards the end of cooking—the stew should be moist but not too liquidy. Serve.

Stuffed Hot Green Peppers

*Stuffed fresh hot green chilies are a popular side dish, especially with **shiro**, the creamy purée made from ground chickpeas or peas. The warmth of the **shiro**—and the tartness of the **injera**—perfectly balance the heat of the peppers. (Warning: the heat is addictive and makes you often eat way too many.)*

Anaheim peppers, which are no longer than 6 inches (15 cm), work best here, since jalapeños or serranos are generally too small. The peppers should be stuffed quite full and so, depending on their size, there might be some stuffing left over, or you might need to use a little more onion and tomato mixture.

SERVES 3–4

3 tablespoons sunflower, canola, or other
   mild vegetable oil

1 tablespoon white wine vinegar

1 tablespoon lemon juice

salt and freshly ground black pepper

2 medium onions, finely chopped

2 medium plum tomatoes, peeled, seeded,
   and finely chopped

6–8 fresh Anaheim peppers or other long,
   thin green chili peppers

In a small bowl, make a vinaigrette by whisking together the oil, vinegar, and lemon juice and seasoning with salt and black pepper. Or simply shake the ingredients together in a sealed jar.

In a large mixing bowl, place the onions and tomatoes, pour over the vinaigrette, and toss to combine.

Wearing rubber gloves, slit open the peppers in a T-shape along the length of one side. Using a teaspoon, carefully remove and discard the seeds. Holding the flaps open with the spoon, fill the peppers with the onion and tomato mixture until quite full. Arrange on a platter and serve.

Shiro Salad

*Creamy, pasty **shiro** (see page 103), made from a ground blend of dried legumes and spices, is Ethiopian comfort food par excellence. But chilled, cut into cubes, breaded, and fried, it brings a tantalizing hint of spice and a lovely contrast of texture to this modern salad.*

SERVES 6

1 cup (250 ml) whole milk

⅔ cup (3 oz/80 g) *mitten shiro* flour (page 103) or chickpea flour

2 tablespoons olive oil

⅔ cup (2½ oz/70 g) teff flour, or more as needed

2 large eggs, whisked

½ cup (2¼ oz/60 g) dried breadcrumbs, or more as needed (made from day-old *injera* or sourdough)

sunflower, canola, or other mild vegetable oil, for frying

1¾ cups (1¾ oz/50 g) fresh tender *moringa* leaves or spinach leaves, finely chopped

1–2 tablespoons finely chopped garlic

1–2 tablespoons grated or finely chopped ginger

1 large or 2 medium *injera* (page 20)

4 tablespoons (2 oz/60 g) butter, melted

lettuce leaves, such as *batavia*, torn into small pieces

2 oz (60 g) feta cheese, cut into cubes or crumbled

To garnish

a handful of grapes, cut in half

a handful of radishes, thinly sliced crossways

a handful of plum tomatoes, quartered lengthways

1 green pepper, seeded and finely chopped

For the vinaigrette

¼ cup (60 ml) olive oil

2 teaspoons freshly squeezed lemon juice

1 teaspoon balsamic vinegar

1 teaspoon finely chopped parsley (optional)

salt and freshly ground black pepper

In a saucepan, heat the milk over medium heat. As soon as it reaches a boil, gradually whisk in the *shiro* flour until you have a thick, creamy paste. Cook, stirring, for about 3 minutes until it gives off roasted aromas, then stir in the olive oil and remove from the heat. Place in a square container about 6 inches (15 cm) wide, allow to cool, and then refrigerate until thoroughly chilled. Turn out onto a chopping board and cut into 1 inch (2.5 cm) cubes.

Place the teff flour in one bowl, the eggs in another, and the breadcrumbs in a third. Roll the cubes first in the flour, then in the eggs, and finally in the breadcrumbs.

In a sauté pan, heat at least ½ inch (1.5 cm) of sunflower oil until the surface shimmers, then reduce the heat to medium. Working in batches so as not to reduce the temperature of the oil, fry the *shiro* cubes for 15–30 seconds until golden, turning as needed. Lift out with a slotted spoon and place on paper towels to drain.

Preheat the oven to 325°F (160°C).

In a small bowl, blend the *moringa*, garlic, and ginger. Brush the top of the *injera* with butter and evenly spread the *moringa* mixture on top. Place on a baking tray, mixture-side up, and toast until crispy. Remove from the oven and set aside to cool before breaking or slicing into six even pieces.

Divide the toasted *injera* between six plates and top with the lettuce leaves. Arrange the garnish ingredients on top and place the feta cheese and *shiro* cubes around the side.

In a small bowl, whisk together the vinaigrette ingredients or shake everything together in a jar. Drizzle over the salad and serve.

5

Legumes
& Grains

Yellow Split Peas in a Mild Ginger and Onion Sauce

In Addis Ababa's Shola market, large burlap bags hold the diverse range of legumes found in the Ethiopian kitchen: chickpeas, small brown fava beans, small round lentils, soy beans, whole dried peas, and split peas.

*When sourcing yellow split peas, note that Indian **toor dal** (pigeon peas) look deceptively similar and **chana dal** look similar but are actually split gram (or chickpeas). Yellow (and green) split peas are field peas, and this is what you want for this recipe.*

SERVES 4

- 1¼ cups (9 oz/250 g) split peas, preferably yellow
- ¼ cup (60 ml) sunflower, canola, or other mild vegetable oil
- 2 medium red or yellow onions, finely chopped (about 9 oz/250 g)
- ½ tablespoon finely chopped garlic
- ½ tablespoon grated or finely chopped ginger
- ¼ teaspoon ground turmeric
- ¼ teaspoon ground ajowan
- salt
- 1 jalapeño pepper, sliced lengthways in half and seeded, to garnish

Place the split peas in a large bowl, pick over, and discard any debris. Rinse and drain.

Bring a large saucepan of water to a boil, add the split peas, and boil, partly covered, for 45–60 minutes until tender. Drain in a colander or sieve, reserving the liquid.

Place a large sauté pan over medium–low heat, add the oil and onions, then cook for about 10 minutes until soft and translucent. Add the garlic and ginger and cook for 1 minute until aromatic. Stir in the turmeric and ajowan, cover, and cook over low heat for 10 minutes. Add a touch of water if needed to keep the sauce from scorching.

Add the split peas and mash lightly with a ladle or the back of a serving spoon, if desired. Season with salt, add ¾ cup (175 ml) of the reserved liquid, and cook for 5–10 minutes until slightly mushy. Add a touch more liquid if needed—the consistency should be loose and saucy but not too runny. Remove from the heat, garnish with the jalapeño, and serve.

Smooth Shiro

Mitten means "balanced" in Amharic, and the blend of legume flour with dry herbs and seasoning refers to the well-adjusted level of spicing used in preparing the powder. Exactly which legumes go into the blend ranges from region to region, but can include chickpeas, fava beans, and/or green peas. The spices can vary greatly, too. I love this recipe, since I find that the garlic and onion revive the flavors of some of the dried ingredients.

*Traditionally, preparing **shiro** powder takes days, and includes roasting and removing the skins of the legumes, adding a range of fresh and dry spices, and milling, but a quick version can be prepared using readily available chickpea flour. In a dry frying pan over low heat, toast ¾ cup (2 ¼ oz/65 g) flour until lightly brown and, while still warm, blend it with 1 tablespoon **berbere** spice blend (see page 40), ½ teaspoon ground cardamom, ½ teaspoon ground nigella seeds, and ½ teaspoon ground ajowan.*

*There are two ways to incorporate **shiro** with onions in the pan. The first, as with the **shiro wat** recipe on page 115, works the dry powder into the onions and then begins working in water. This recipe, however, uses an alternative method and whisks the powder with water into a smooth paste before adding it to the pot.*

Serve with chilled stuffed green peppers (see page 97).

SERVES 2–4

½ cup (2¼ oz/65 g) *mitten shiro* flour

1 tablespoon sunflower, canola, or other mild vegetable oil

¼ medium red or yellow onion, finely chopped

2 teaspoons finely chopped garlic

1 teaspoon grated or finely chopped ginger

salt

½ tablespoon *niter kebbeh* (page 52) or clarified butter, or more to taste

¼ jalapeño pepper, seeded and chopped, to garnish

In a bowl, whisk the *shiro* powder with 2 cups (500 ml) of hot water to a smooth, runny paste without any lumps.

In a saucepan, heat the oil over medium heat, add the onion, garlic, and ginger, and cook for 1 minute until aromatic. Pour in the shiro paste, stir, and season with salt. Cook, covered, for about 20 minutes, stirring frequently and adding more hot water as needed to keep the mixture smooth. It should result in a creamy, pudding-like consistency and have lost any raw taste or sense of grittiness. Stir in the *niter kebbeh* and spoon into a serving bowl. Garnish with jalapeños and serve.

Lenten Lentil Salad with Mustard

This chilled lentil salad, from the highland of Amhara, is especially popular during the long Lenten fast. However, it also makes a delicious appetizer or part of a multi-dish meal at any time of the year. As one of the few "cold" dishes in the country, it offers a lovely contrast to others, particularly the spicy ones, on the table.

Use green lentils or small brown ones (sometimes called Spanish or pardina), and boil until only just tender—don't allow them to get mushy. Some cooks prepare this recipe without mustard, but a good dollop of strong mustard, ideally homemade Ethiopian **senafich** *(page 54), gives it a lovely tang.*

SERVES 4

1¼ cups (9 oz/250 g) dried small whole green or brown lentils

2 teaspoons mustard, preferably homemade Ethiopian brown mustard (page 54)

½ medium yellow onion, finely chopped

1 small jalapeño pepper, seeded and finely chopped

3–4 tablespoons sunflower, canola, or other mild vegetable oil

1 small lemon, cut in half

salt

Place the lentils in a large bowl and pick over and discard any debris. Rinse and drain.

Bring a large saucepan of water to a boil, add the lentils, and boil for 25–30 minutes until just tender. Drain in a colander or sieve. If desired, mash lightly with a ladle or the back of a serving spoon and then transfer to a large salad bowl. Once completely cool, cover with plastic wrap and refrigerate until chilled.

Before serving, add the mustard, onion, jalapeño, and oil, squeeze over the lemon, and season with salt. Toss well and serve chilled.

Lentil Soup with Spicy Dried Beef and Crispy Leeks

*Quanta are dried strips of beef rubbed in **berbere**. You can also use good-quality beef jerky as a substitute (although not the type that has been made from ground meat and shaped into a tube) and toss it first with some **berbere** to give it a jolt of flavor. Note that the dried meat isn't cooked until soft; rather, its pleasant chewiness contrasts nicely with the texture of the soup.*

SERVES 6

4–6 oz (115–170 g) Ethiopian *quanta* or artisanal dried beef jerky

4 tablespoons sunflower, canola, or other mild vegetable oil, plus more for frying

berbere spice blend (page 40)

salt and freshly ground black pepper

2 cups (14 oz/400 g) dried small brown or green lentils

1 medium red or yellow onion, finely chopped

¾ cup (175 ml) passata or tomato sauce

generous 3 cups (750 ml) chicken stock

2 medium leeks, washed

Cut the *quanta* or beef jerky into bite-size pieces. Moisten with 1 tablespoon of the oil and lightly toss with *berbere*, salt, and black pepper to taste. Set aside.

Place the lentils in a large bowl and pick over, discarding any debris. Rinse and drain.

In a medium Dutch oven, combine the beef jerky with 2 tablespoons of the oil and cook for 1 minute to flavor and color the oil. Remove the jerky and set aside. Add the onion and cook for a few seconds, stirring continuously, to blend the flavor. Add the lentils and the remaining 1 tablespoon of oil, stir in the passata, and cook for 2–3 minutes, stirring well.

Pour in the stock and a generous 3 cups (750 ml) of water, season with salt, and bring to a boil. Reduce the heat to medium-low, partly cover, and simmer for 30–40 minutes until the lentils are tender. Add more water if necessary to keep the mixture loose. Remove from the heat.

Meanwhile, trim the leeks, discarding the roots and tough green tops, and remove the outer layer or two. Slice each leek crossways into two pieces about 2 inches (5 cm) long and then cut each piece lengthways into thin slivers.

In a medium frying pan, heat at least ½ inch (1.5 cm) of oil until the surface shimmers, then reduce the heat to medium. Working in batches so as not to crowd the pan, fry the leeks for about 5 minutes until brown and chewy-crispy. Using a slotted spoon, transfer them to paper towels to drain.

Return the jerky to the pot and stir to warm it through, then ladle into bowls. Scatter the crispy leeks on top of each bowl and serve.

Harar & Muslim Ethiopia

Home to 82 mosques and 102 Muslim shrines,[1] the walled city of Harar, some 300 miles east of Addis Ababa, is known as Madinatal Aouliya, "City of Saints."[2] UNESCO has dated three of those mosques to the tenth century,[3] about the time of Harar's founding. Considered the fourth holiest city in Islam, it was long off-limits to non-believers. The first infidel to enter its gates was the English explorer and linguist Richard Burton in 1854, when the city was already nearly a thousand years old. In January 1887, after being ruled by a successive line of emirs from AD 969–1886, the city-state was defeated by the ruler Menelik II and incorporated into the expanding Ethiopian Empire.

As a transit point for Muslims in Ethiopia making the Islamic Hajj, or annual pilgrimage to Mecca, Harar was a key link to the Arabian Peninsula and to Islam. It remains the spiritual heart of the country's Muslim community, along with Argobba, where it is said Islam first settled as Yifat civilization in Abyssinia, the former name of Ethiopia. About one-third of Ethiopia's population is Muslim, largely in the outlying areas and especially to the east (including Afar, see page 9), with their own strong culinary traditions, dietary restrictions, and annual period of fasting (see page 93). While Orthodox Christians abstain from meat and dairy products during their fasts, Muslims forgo all food and drink from sunrise to sunset during the month of Ramadan.

Today in Harar, all religions live together in perfect harmony. Within the city walls, less than 100 yards apart, the Orthodox church, the Catholic church, and the oldest mosque (see opposite top left, bottom left, top right respectively) chant turn by turn, charming their followers who have long embraced their differences and shown a greater cultural bond.

In the past, Harar was a main commercial center in the Horn of Africa, an important trading post and stop for caravans traveling between the Ethiopian highlands and the ports of Zeila and Berbera. Harar's markets were famed for their ivory, musk, spices, leather, and even ostrich feathers. And, of course, their coffee.

Grown on the dry hills outside the city, Harar's coffee continues to be celebrated for its exceptional quality. Offering a mild, creamy brew, with classic hints of chocolate, wine, and blueberries, it fetches the highest prices of any region at the official coffee exchange in Addis Ababa.

In the narrow alleys of the dense old city "Jegol," or in markets tucked alongside its ancient ramparts, one finds plenty of stalls offering the famous coffee beans. Vendors also sell vegetables grown in the hills around the city, camel meat, local sorghum, teff, and *luban*, high-quality incense from Somalia that locals burn during the coffee ceremony. And there are plenty of fragrant spices, too. Fenugreek (*abish*) is particularly popular here and cooks in the Adere culture use it with gusto in meat stews such as *abish wat* (page 132).

And there is also another hugely popular local crop, *khat*. This mildly narcotic leaf is chewed fresh to enhance concentration and conversations. Harar, like Dire Dawa—famous for its sweets, is a hot city and many there give their afternoons over to *khat*. Slowly feeding the tender leaves into their mouths, they wait for the hyena feeding ritual.

Traditionally, hyena feeding is a superstitious belief following the Ramadan season for Ashura. Harari's prepare *genfo* (see page 58) to feed hyenas and particularly the "Dermeshake" (the matriarch), whose feasting is considered a sign of prosperity for the upcoming year. Hyena feeding is such an esteemed culture in Harar that 10 extra miniature doors, in addition to the 5 main gates on the Harar wall, were built in the seventeenth century exclusively to welcome hyenas into the city, allowing them to eat the wasted food they find. Today, tourism has fiddled its practice, making it an everyday feeding ritual at the outskirts of the city, that many, in the evenings, enjoy by petting the semi-domesticated beasts.

---

1. https://whc.unesco.org/en/list/1189
2. David Vo Van, Mohammed Jami Guleid, *Harar: A Cultural Guide* (Shama Books)
3. https://whc.unesco.org/en/list/1189

Kidney Bean and Okra Stew with Cornmeal Patties

*In Gambela, the far west of Ethiopia along the South Sudan border, there are five ethnic groups: the Opo, Gnuer, Agnuak, Komo, and Mejeng. While all use **genfo** as the staple food of Gambela, each have a specialized and particular way of preparing it, which in turn creates major variations in texture, appearance, and taste.*

*This dish is a speciality of the Komo. For this okra and bean stew, cooks not only grind the peanuts into a paste but also roast and grind the corn used to make a **genfo**-like dough to eat with it. This recipe simplifies the work by calling for peanut butter and preparing the corn dough with fine yellow cornmeal. To eat, pinch off a piece of dough, flatten into a small patty, and use it to scoop up the stew.*

SERVES 4

1 lb (450 g) okra, ends trimmed and cut
   crossways into ½ inch (1 cm) pieces

2 medium plum tomatoes, cored and chopped

salt

14 oz (400 g) can cooked kidney beans, drained

2 tablespoons finely chopped fresh hot green
   chilies, such as bird's eye or jalapeño, or more
   to taste

2 tablespoons finely chopped fresh *besobela*
   (page 38) or Thai basil (optional)

¼ cup (2¼ oz/65 g) creamy unsalted peanut
   butter

2½ cups (11 oz/320 g) fine yellow cornmeal

In a large saucepan, bring 3 cups (700 ml) of water to a boil. Add the okra and tomatoes, season with salt, and cook for 15–20 minutes until the okra is soft and the liquid a bit viscous. Add the beans and cook for 5 minutes.

Pound the chilies and *besobela* (if using) into a paste using a mortar and pestle or purée using a food processor, adding in a touch of water if needed. Transfer to a bowl and whisk in the peanut butter and about 1 cup (250 ml) of the simmering liquid (if you get a few beans, it's OK) until you have a runny paste. Return the mixture to the pan and cook for 1–2 minutes, stirring continuously. Add a touch more water if needed—the mixture should be quite loose but not watery. Taste for seasoning and set aside.

In a large saucepan, bring 3 cups (700 ml) of water to a boil and slowly stir in the cornmeal with a wooden spoon, working it for about 3 minutes until you have a thick, smooth mass of dough that holds its shape. Moisten a deep soup bowl with water, place the cornmeal mixture in it, and shake the bowl in a rotating circular manner until the mixture forms a smooth, round ball.

To serve, place the stew in a serving bowl. To eat, pinch off a piece of corn dough, flatten it to form a small patty, and use it to scoop up the stew.

Spicy Chickpea Flour Stew

Shiro *is a tasty stew that can be presented in many ways. It was a dish for the common man but today is seen as one of the identifying dishes of Ethiopia, eaten by all. Chickpeas, peas, and/or beans are boiled with a range of seasonings, dried in the sun or roasted, and then ground. This flour-like powder is then cooked into a smooth, thick, creamy paste with onions, clarified butter, and spices. Many Ethiopian food shops worldwide stock the main types of* **shiro** *powder, from the ivory* **netch Shiro** *to the reddish* **berbere**-blend **Mitten Shiro** *(see page 103).*

Along with a range of flavors, these stews vary in consistencies. **Shiro fessess** *is the runniest—***fessess** *means "runny" in Amharic—and is prepared by thinning* **shiro wat** *and then serving it very hot on top of* **injera** *with jalapeños on the side. Conversely,* **shiro tegabino** *is reduced in a small clay pot until the bottom starts to caramelize and stick. The recipe below occupies a middle ground and produces a creamy stew that should hold its form. Note, though, that bubbling* **shiro** *has a tendency to splatter so be careful when stirring, especially towards the end of cooking.*

Milad shiro *is the last version of a* **shiro** *meal and is directly cooked on* **mitad** *(see page 10), which consequently affects the shiro's final texture and taste. This recipe, largely practiced around Bahir Dar, is a simple mix of* **shiro** *powder with cold water and cooked on* **milad** *for 3 minutes. This process brings the thickest form of* **shiro wot,** *which also makes it the hottest in term of spice intensity sensed in the mouth.*

SERVES 2–4

3 tablespoons sunflower, canola, or other mild oil

¼ medium red or yellow onion, finely chopped

½ tablespoon finely chopped garlic

½ cup (2¼ oz/65 g) *shiro wat* flour

salt

½ tablespoon *niter kebbeh* (page 52) or clarified butter

In a large saucepan, bring a generous 3 cups (750 ml) of water to a boil and keep hot.

In another large saucepan, heat the oil over medium heat, add the onion and garlic, and cook for about 1 minute until aromatic. Sprinkle in the *shiro* flour and cook for a further minute, stirring continuously, until it begins to smell a bit nutty.

Begin working in 2 cups (500 ml) of the hot water, stirring with a whisk. Cook, covered, for about 30 minutes, stirring frequently and adding more hot water as needed—it should be creamy and have lost any raw taste or sense of grittiness. Season with salt, stir in the *niter kebbeh*, ladle into a serving bowl, and serve.

Chickpeas with Spicy Flaxseed Paste

This dish comes from Lalibela—one-time imperial capital and home to eleven magnificent monolithic churches hewn from a single rock some nine hundred years ago. It is also a place where chickpeas, the Desi variety in particular, are extremely popular. Cooking the **awaze** *before blending it with the legumes tempers the chili-rich sauce's heat. Ideally, serve with* **injera**, *which will soak up the ample rust-red sauce.*

SERVES 3–4

3 tablespoons brown or golden flaxseed

3 tablespoons *awaze* dipping sauce (page 45)

14 oz (400 g) cooked or canned chickpeas, drained and rinsed

salt

Dry-toast and grind the flaxseed following the instructions on page 66 (*telba fitfit*).

In a Dutch oven or sauté pan, heat 2 tablespoons of water over low heat and stir in 1 tablespoon of the *awaze*. Cook for 2 minutes, stirring continuously, then gradually work in the remaining 2 tablespoons of *awaze*, along with the ground flaxseed and 1 cup (250 ml) of water. Reduce the heat to its lowest possible level, cover, and cook, stirring frequently, for 20 minutes. Add a touch more water if it looks like the mixture is drying out—it should still be a bit runny at the end.

Meanwhile, place the chickpeas in a saucepan and cover with 2 cups (500 ml) of water. Bring to a boil, remove from the heat, and soak in the liquid until ready to use. Drain the chickpeas, reserving about 1 cup (240 ml) of the liquid. Add the chickpeas to the *awaze*-flaxseed mixture, generously season with salt, and mix well. Tip in some of the reserved cooking water if needed so that the sauce is a touch runny and evenly coats the chickpeas. Cook for a couple of minutes to combine the flavors before serving.

Spicy Red Lentils

*This spicy red lentil dish is a staple of the Ethiopian kitchen. Traditionally, it contains a fair amount of **berbere** but I find that by adding just a pinch of this chili-based spice blend, the lovely earthiness of the onion base and nigella comes through. It makes for a milder— but far from bland—version of the dish for those desiring something less spicy.*

* **Misr wat** is one of those stews that is tastier once it has been taken off the stove and allowed to rest for a while. Reheat just before serving.*

SERVES 4

1¼ cups (9 oz/250 g) dried split red lentils

¼ cup (60 ml) sunflower, canola, or other mild vegetable oil

2 medium red or yellow onions, finely chopped (about 9 oz/250 g)

½ tablespoon finely chopped garlic

2 teaspoons *berbere* spice blend (page 40), or more to taste

½ teaspoon ground nigella seeds

salt

½ teaspoon *mekelesha* spice blend (page 44) (optional)

Place the lentils in a large bowl and pick over and discard any debris. Rinse and drain.

Bring a large saucepan of water to a boil, add the lentils, and boil for about 12 minutes until just tender. Drain in a colander or sieve, reserving the liquid. Mash lightly with a ladle or the back of a serving spoon.

Meanwhile, heat a large sauté pan or wide saucepan over medium–low heat. Add the oil and onions and cook for about 10 minutes until soft and translucent. Add the garlic and cook for 1 minute until aromatic. Stir in the *berbere* and nigella, cover, and cook over low heat for 10 minutes. Add a touch of water to keep it from scorching.

Add the lentils, season with salt, and cook for 5 minutes, stirring frequently. Loosen with about ½ cup (125 ml) of the reserved liquid, season with the *mekelesha* (if using), and cook, uncovered, over medium heat for another few minutes. Set aside until needed and reheat before serving.

Ethiopian Gnocchi

*Beso is the name for flour that has been milled from roasted barley and is used in an array of Ethiopian dishes, including snacks such as **chicko** (see page 205). However, a little confusingly, it is also the name for flour that has been milled from roasted wheat and so, drawing on that tradition, this modern recipe uses pan-roasted flour to bring a nutty flavor to gnocchi-shaped fresh "pasta."*

SERVES 6

1²/₃ cups (7 oz/200 g) plus 3 tablespoons all-purpose flour

3¾ cups (900 ml) whole milk

6 tablespoons (3 oz/80 g) plus 3 tablespoons (1½ oz/40 g) unsalted butter

½ whole nutmeg, freshly grated

1 pinch *mitmita* spice blend (page 47)

4 large eggs

salt and white pepper

scant 1 cup (3½ oz/100 g) freshly grated mild cheese, such as Gouda or Gruyère

In a dry frying pan, toast the flour for 10–15 minutes until golden brown. Transfer to a bowl.

In a large saucepan, add 1¾ cups (420 ml) of the milk and 6 tablespoons (3 oz/80 g) of the butter, season with nutmeg and *mitmita,* and bring to a simmer. Mix in 1²/₃ cups (7 oz/200 g) of the flour and cook for about 3 minutes, stirring frequently, until the mixture reaches the consistency of a light pastry dough.

Transfer the dough to a stand mixer. Mixing the dough on a low speed, add in the eggs, one at a time. Alternatively, mix by hand: transfer the dough to a mixing bowl, stir for a few minutes to cool, and then begin adding the eggs one by one, vigorously stirring to thoroughly incorporate before adding the next one.

Transfer the dough to a pastry bag fitted with a plain ½ inch (1.5 cm) tip.

Bring a large pot of salted water to a boil and, holding the pastry bag over the pot, squeeze out the pastry, cutting with scissors at 1 inch (2.5 cm) intervals, and allowing the gnocchi to fall into the water. Cook for a few minutes until they start to float, then transfer with a slotted spoon to a bowl of iced water. Once they have fallen to the bottom, remove them from the water and spread them out on a plate to dry.

Preheat the oven to 400°F (200°C). Warm the remaining 2 cups (480 ml) milk and set aside.

In a saucepan, melt the remaining 3 tablespoons of butter over medium–low heat and stir in the remaining 3 tablespoons of flour. Reduce the heat to low and cook, stirring, for 1–2 minutes until it looks and smells a little toasted. Whisk in the reserved hot milk and cook over low heat, stirring continuously, for about 5 minutes and until it thickly coats the back of a spoon—you should have about 1¾ cups (420 ml) of béchamel sauce. Season with salt and white pepper.

In a baking dish, stir the gnocchi and sauce to thoroughly coat, then transfer to the oven and bake for about 15 minutes until bubbly and hot. Generously spread the cheese over the top and place the dish under the broiler until the cheese is melted and golden. Serve.

Moringa Teff Lasagne

*The selection of pasta in Addis Ababa supermarkets is the largest of any product, probably due to our history with Italy in the 1930s. This modern take on lasagna uses **moringa**, a nutritious herb. In the south of Ethiopia, **moringa** is best known as **sheferawu** or **haleko** and used as a natural medicine in **fosesse**, a traditional tabbouleh-like recipe with freshly chopped **moringa**. In Europe it is mostly dried as green tea and herbal medicine. As dried versions tend to be bitter, substitute fresh tender spinach leaves here instead. The dish reduces the amount of gluten by blending wheat flour with the flour of teff (see pages 16–17).*

SERVES 4

2 cups (6 oz/175 g) grated mozzarella cheese

1½ cups (350 ml) tomato sauce, preferably
  homemade

For the pasta dough

scant 1½ cups (5¾ oz/165 g) teff flour

1¼ cups (5½ oz/150 g) all-purpose flour,
  plus extra for dusting

3 large eggs

2½ tablespoons olive oil

For the *moringa* béchamel

2 tablespoons unsalted butter

2 tablespoons all-purpose flour

1¼ cups (300 ml) whole milk, warmed

1 garlic clove, roughly chopped

12 oz (350 g) fresh tender *moringa* leaves
  or spinach leaves

salt and freshly ground black pepper

In a bowl, combine the teff flour and the all-purpose flour. Tip the combined flours onto a clean work surface in a large mound and make a well in the middle. Crack the eggs into the well and add 1½ tablespoons of oil. Begin mixing in the flour from the sides until gradually incorporated into a single ball. Knead the dough until supple, dusting with all-purpose flour if needed. Cover the dough with a wet cloth and set aside to rest for 30 minutes.

Dust a clean work surface with flour and divide the dough into four equal balls. Working with one at a time, press into a flat disc, then flatten each disk thinly (about 1.5 mm) using a rolling pin. Cut each stretched sheet into rectangular lasagne pieces and sprinkle with all-purpose flour.

Bring a large pot of salted water to boil. Add the pasta sheets one by one and cook for 5 minutes, or until al dente. Transfer to a bowl of cold water, then drain.

Make the béchamel sauce. In a saucepan, melt the butter over medium–low heat and then stir in the 2 tablespoons of flour. Reduce the heat and cook, stirring, for 1–2 minutes until it looks and smells a little toasted. Gradually whisk in the warm milk until it thickly coats the back of a spoon—you should have about 1 cup (240 ml) of béchamel.

In a clean sauté pan over medium heat, add the remaining 1 tablespoon of oil, garlic, and *moringa*, season with salt, cover, and cook for 5 minutes until the *moringa* has wilted and is tender. Remove from the heat. Place the *moringa* and ½ cup (125 ml) of the béchamel in a food processor and purée—you should have about 1¼ cups (300 ml) of *moringa* sauce. Season with salt and black pepper.

Preheat the oven to 400°F (200°C). Grease the bottom and sides of a baking dish and place a layer of lasagne sheets across the bottom. Spread ¼ cup (60 ml) of the *moringa* sauce over the top, sprinkle with ⅓–½ cup (1–1½ oz/30–40 g) of the cheese, and then spread a thin layer of tomato sauce on top. Repeat this layering four times. However, for the top layer, reverse the order so that you finish with the *moringa* sauce.

Bake for about 15 minutes until the cheese has melted and the lasagne is heated through. Serve with a grind of black pepper.

Teff Tagliatelle with Sprouted Fenugreek and Carrots

Fenugreek is a beloved spice in Ethiopia, especially in Harar where 3 varieties can be found. Cooks there use different techniques for tempering its natural bitterness. One of them is washing and sprouting the seeds, and this modern pasta dish uses sprouted fenugreek to bring a hint of earthiness to the creamy sauce, which beautifully balances the sweetness of the carrots. You can also add a few chopped sun-dried tomatoes to give the sauce a little extra color and complexity. However, it's important that you plan ahead since you need to allow a couple of days for the seeds to sprout.

SERVES 4

1 tablespoon whole fenugreek seeds

1 tablespoon butter

a sprig of fresh thyme

3 small-medium carrots, peeled and cut into bite-size lengths

2½ cups (600 ml) chicken stock

1 cup (240 ml) light cream

1 heaped tablespoon blue cheese

salt and freshly ground black pepper

3 oz (85 g) pitted black olives

For the pasta dough

scant 1½ cups (5¾ oz/165 g) teff flour

1¼ cups (5½ oz/150 g) all-purpose flour, plus more for dusting

3 large eggs

1½ tablespoons olive oil

Sprout the fenugreek seeds first. Place them in a glass jar, cover with a piece of mesh netting, and secure with a rubber band. Fill the jar with water and soak for 6–8 hours. Drain, rinse, and drain again. Place the jar in the light and keep for two days until sprouts appear, rinsing and draining the seeds twice a day. Rinse a final time and spread out on a plate to dry.

For the pasta dough, pile the flours on a clean work surface and make a well in the center. Crack the eggs into the well, add the olive oil, and gradually mix in the flour from the sides until a ball forms. Knead the dough until supple, dusting with all-purpose flour if needed. Cover with a wet cloth and set aside to rest for 30 minutes.

Dust a clean work surface with flour and divide the dough into four equal balls. Working with one at a time, press into a disc, then roll out each disk thinly (about 1.5 mm). Either cut by hand or use a pasta machine. To cut by hand, flour both sides of each sheet and loosely roll up into a cylinder. With a sharp knife, cut strips ¼ inch (5 mm) wide and unravel, dusting with all-purpose flour. Gently lay on floured dish towels. Repeat with the remaining dough and set aside.

In a large saucepan over medium heat, melt the butter, add the thyme, and sear the carrots all over. Add 1 cup (250 ml) of the stock and cook, partly covered, for 10 minutes. Remove from the heat when almost completely dry. Set aside and cover.

Place another large saucepan over medium heat. Add the remaining stock and boil to reduce by half. Stir in the cream and blue cheese, then simmer until it has a sauce consistency. Season with salt and pepper. Remove from the heat, add the olives, carrots, and 2–3 tablespoons of the fenugreek, and set aside to infuse for 10 minutes.

Bring a large pot of salted water to a rolling boil. Add the pasta and cook for 5 minutes until al dente, stirring from time to time to keep the pasta from clumping. Drain, toss with the sauce, and serve.

Beef, Lamb
& Goat

Ground Prime Beef in Spicy Fenugreek Sauce

*Minchet abish—spicy ground beef with fenugreek—is a favorite to serve during festive meals in the Amhara region. This version also includes **shiro**, a spiced legume flour, which adds a little succulence to the dish. Use **nech shiro** (white) or **mitten shiro** ("balanced"; see page 103 for a quick version). If using **shiro wat** (spicy), reduce the amount of **berbere** in the recipe. Ethiopian shops sell **shiro** flours, but chickpea flour will also work as a quick substitution in this recipe.*

SERVES 4

3 tablespoons sunflower, canola, or other mild vegetable oil

1 medium red or yellow onion, finely chopped

½ teaspoon ground fenugreek

1 tablespoon finely chopped garlic

½ tablespoon grated or finely chopped ginger

1 tablespoon *berbere* spice blend (page 40), or more to taste

½ cup (125 ml) *tej* (pages 172–173), or medium dry white wine whisked with ½ tablespoon honey

8 oz (225 g) lean ground or finely chopped beef

4 tablespoons *niter kebbeh* (page 52) or clarified butter

1 teaspoon ground nigella seeds

salt

2 tablespoons *shiro* or chickpea flour

¼ teaspoon ground *mekelesha* spice blend (page 44), or more to taste

Place a heavy-bottomed saucepan over medium–low heat. Add the oil, onion, and fenugreek and cook, stirring frequently, for 8–10 minutes until soft and golden. Add the garlic and ginger and cook for about a minute, until aromatic. Stir in the *berbere*, ¼ cup (60 ml) of the *tej*, cover, and cook for 10 minutes, stirring frequently. Add a touch of water if needed to keep it from scorching.

Add the ground beef, 2 tablespoons of the *niter kebbeh*, and the nigella, season with salt, and cook, stirring frequently, for about 5 minutes until the meat is browned. Add the remaining ¼ cup (60 ml) of *tej* and simmer uncovered for 5 minutes.

Whisk the *shiro* into ½ cup (125 ml) of hot water until smooth and without lumps and then stir into the pot. Cover almost entirely with a lid and cook over low heat, stirring frequently, for about 20 minutes, until the *shiro* is thick and smooth and has lost any raw floury taste. Add a bit of hot water if needed to achieve a final consistency that is stewy and moist but not too runny.

Stir in the *mekelesha* and remaining 2 tablespoons of *niter kebbeh*, cook for a final 3–4 minutes, and serve.

Collard Greens with Beef Stew

*This rich and savory stew marries two perfectly matched ingredients—beef and **gomen,** or local collard greens. As with other **gomen** recipes (pages 80 and 82), you can use kale or other spring greens rather than collards, though the stew will need more water and a slightly longer cooking time for them to become tender. Traditionally, retaining the chlorophyll of the greens is not valued thus this dish is cooked covered to reach the desired meat and leaf texture.*

SERVES 3–4

¼ cup (60 ml) sunflower, canola, or other mild vegetable oil

4 medium red or yellow onions, finely chopped (about 1 lb 2 oz/500 g)

1 tablespoon finely chopped garlic

1 teaspoon grated or finely chopped ginger

mitmita spice blend (page 47)

1 lb 2 oz (500 g) stewing beef, cut into pieces about 1 x 1½ inches (2.5 x 4 cm)

1 lb 2 oz (500 g) beef bones

2¼ lb (1 kg) fresh collard greens or kale

salt

2 tablespoons *niter kebbeh* (page 52) or clarified butter

Place a large sauté pan or wide saucepan over medium heat. Add the oil and onions and cook for 10–15 minutes until soft and translucent. Stir in the garlic and ginger and cook for about 1 minute until aromatic. Season with *mitmita* and add the beef and bones. Cover and cook over low heat for 30–40 minutes, stirring from time to time. Add a touch of water if needed to keep it from scorching.

Meanwhile, wash the greens in warm, salted water and then drain. Trim the fibrous stems and, if desired, the tough center veins. Cut the leaves crossways into 1 inch (2.5 cm) wide strips. There should be about 1 lb 2 oz (500 g) of prepared greens.

Add the greens to the pot, season with salt, cover, and cook for about 30 minutes until the greens and meat are tender. Add a touch of water if needed during cooking. Stir in the *niter kebbeh* and serve.

Cubed Sirloin with Onions and Jalapeño Peppers

*The name **shekla** refers to the two-tiered, crown-shaped clay dish used to serve this popular beef dish. In the bottom of the pot are embers that keep the meat warm and traditionally, people cooked the meat in rendered beef fat (tallow). Serve with **injera**.*

SERVES 4

2 ¼ lb (1 kg) lean beef, such as top round or sirloin, cut into 1 inch (2.5 cm) cubes
salt and freshly ground black pepper
sunflower, canola, or other mild vegetable oil, for frying
2 medium yellow onions, thinly sliced and separated
1 jalapeño pepper, seeded and thinly sliced
awaze dipping sauce (page 45)

Season the beef with salt and black pepper.

In a sauté pan, heat at least ½ inch (1.5 cm) of oil until the surface shimmers, then reduce the heat to medium. Working in batches so that you do not reduce the temperature of the oil, gently place the meat in the oil and fry for 1–2 minutes, depending on the desired level of doneness. Transfer with a slotted spoon to paper towels to drain. Fry the remaining meat.

Arrange the meat in a *shekla* pot or serving bowl and season with salt if needed. Sprinkle over the onions and jalapeño and serve immediately with a dish of *awaze* on the side for dipping.

Sizzling Beef Strips with Awaze Chili Sauce

*Zilzil refers to meat that has been cut into long strips using a technique that unfurls a chunk of meat into a somewhat imperfect strip. Using a good piece of top round or sirloin makes a tasty—and certainly quicker—version of this favorite dish. Serve with a fine Ethiopian beer, such as St. George, Bedele, Meta, Habesha, or **tella**, the local traditional beer variety. And plenty of **injera**, of course.*

* **Awaze** is generally served as a dipping sauce but here, uniquely, it is used as an ingredient.*

SERVES 2

1 lb (450 g) lean beef, such as top round or
   sirloin, cut into thin ½ inch (1 cm) wide strips
salt
sunflower, canola, or other mild vegetable
   oil, for greasing the pan
½ tablespoon *awaze* dipping sauce (page 45),
   or more to taste
½ tablespoon *niter kebbeh* (page 52)
   or clarified butter

Season the meat with salt.

Heat a heavy-bottomed frying pan over high heat and lightly grease the pan with oil. Working in batches, add the meat and sear for 1–2 minutes on each side, then transfer to a plate.

Once the meat has been seared, return all of the meat to the pan, stir in the *awaze* and *niter kebbeh*, and cook, turning regularly, for 1–2 minutes until the meat is done.

Transfer to an earthenware serving bowl or plate and serve immediately.

Fried Beef with Onions

Popular and prepared all year round by those who don't fast, this dish even manages to find a place on the Orthodox Christian fast-breaking Easter and Christmas tables. Use the largest frying pan you have and move the onions to the outside of the pan once they are done and then sear the pieces of meat in small batches in the center, moving them to the outside with the onions when they are also done.

*For a saucy version of this dish, add a touch of **tej** (mead), wine, or even just a dash of water before the jalapeño and cook for 2 minutes or so, stirring frequently to capture all the flavors in the pan. You can substitute chicken here nicely too.*

*Note that **mitmita** spice blend contains a fair amount of salt so adjust the seasoning of the dish accordingly.*

SERVES 4

3 tablespoons sunflower, canola, or other
   mild vegetable oil

2 medium red or yellow onions, thinly sliced

2¼ lb (1 kg) lean beef, such as top round or
   sirloin, cut into ¾ inch (2 cm) cubes

salt and freshly ground black pepper

1 small sprig of fresh rosemary, destalked and
   finely chopped

1½ tablespoons *niter kebbeh* (page 52) or
   clarified butter

mitmita spice blend (page 47)

1 jalapeño pepper, seeded and sliced crossways

In a large frying pan or sauté pan, heat the oil over medium heat, add the onions, and cook for 10–15 minutes until browned, before moving to the outside of the pan.

Season the beef with salt and black pepper. Increase the heat to medium–high or high and begin cooking the meat with the rosemary in small batches in the center of the pan, for 1 minute or so on each side, before moving to the outside of the pan with the onions when done.

Add the *niter kebbeh*, season with *mitmita*, and stir to blend. Scatter over the jalapeño and remove from the heat.

Serve with a bowl of *mitmita* on the side to dip the meat into, if desired.

Spicy Beef and Fenugreek Stew with Potatoes

Abish or fenugreek is the spice that dominates this dish from Harar. In Ethiopia, the Adere community is well known for its love of **abish** and for having fine skin—two characteristics that some link together.

Before grinding the hard, dark-yellow spice, cooks often go through a laborious process of washing and drying the seeds, roasting and even pounding them together with onions in a mortar before drying and then finally grinding them to a fine powder. This process reduces fenugreek's bitterness but retains its aromas and properties and allows cooks to use large quantities of the spice.

SERVES 4

1 lb 2 oz (500 g) sirloin or top round beef, cut into large cubes

4 ripe medium tomatoes, peeled, cored, and seeded

1 medium red or yellow onion, finely chopped

2 garlic cloves, finely chopped

1 tablespoon ground fenugreek, or more to taste

2 tablespoons *berbere* spice blend (page 40), or more to taste

¼ teaspoon ground cumin

¼ teaspoon ground nigella seeds

4 tablespoons sunflower, canola, or other mild vegetable oil

salt

6 waxy white potatoes, peeled

1 teaspoon *mekelesha* spice mix (page 44)

injera (page 20), to serve

In a large, sauté pan or wide saucepan, place the meat, cover with 6⅓ cups (1.5 liters) of cold water and bring to a simmer. Skim off any foam.

Meanwhile, in a food processor or blender, purée the tomatoes and transfer to a mixing bowl. Add the onion, garlic, fenugreek, *berbere*, cumin, nigella, and oil, and season with salt. Add about ½ cup (125 ml) of the simmering liquid and stir into the mixture. Pour into the pan with the beef and water.

Cover and cook over medium–low heat for 60 minutes. Add the potatoes, making sure they are submerged, and cook for 20–30 minutes, or until the meat and potatoes are both tender. Add the *mekelesha* and cook for a final few minutes. The sauce should be stewy and a little runny.

To serve, ladle some stew into the bottom of a wide serving bowl. Tear some *injera* into large pieces and place in the bowl over the sauce. Ladle the remaining stew over the top of the *injera*. Serve with spoons and the remaining *injera* on the side.

Dried Beef Stew with Onions, Peppers, Spices, and Dried Injera

*Quanta is made using an ancient method of preserving strips of spiced beef using salt from eastern Ethiopia. The meat is coated with a mixture of oil and **berbere**, cut into strips, and hung in the shade to dry. While authentic **quanta** might be hard to find outside Ethiopia, there are many excellent ready-made artisanal types of beef jerky available. Slice it into thin strips, rub them with **berbere**, and oven-dry to get a similar taste to the local **quanta**.*

The dried meat here is not cooked until tender. Rather, it is only in the pan for a few minutes and should retain its chewy texture.

SERVES 2–4

3 tablespoons sunflower, canola, or other mild vegetable oil

2 medium red or white onions, finely chopped (about 9 oz/250 g)

2 garlic cloves, finely chopped

1 tablespoon *berbere* spice blend (page 40)

1 tablespoon *niter kebbeh* (page 52) or clarified butter

4½ oz (125 g) artisanal beef jerky, cut into thin strips about 2 inches (5 cm) long

salt

injera (page 20), oven dried until fully crisp

Place a large frying pan or sauté pan over medium–low heat. Add the oil and onions and cook for about 10 minutes until soft and translucent. Stir in the garlic and cook for about 1 minute until aromatic. Stir in the *berbere* with a couple of spoonfuls of water, cover, and cook over low heat for 15 minutes, stirring frequently. Add a touch more water if needed to keep it from scorching.

Stir in about 1 cup (250 ml) of hot water and bring to a boil. Stir in the *niter kebbeh*, add the dried beef, season with salt, and cook for 1–2 minutes. The meat should still be chewy and the sauce should be fairly runny. Add a bit more water if needed. Spoon into a serving bowl.

Break the dried *injera* into pieces and gently push the pieces into the sauce before servings.

Spicy Beef Stew with Barley Dough

*This specialty from the northern Tigray region comes from around the town of Adigrat, just south of the Eritrea border. Unlike many Ethiopian stews, it doesn't have an onion base and so takes less time to prepare, and the cool sauce and balls of barley dough both help balance the heat of the spices. Usually, a piece of dough is impaled on the end of a short wooden fork-like prong and dipped into the pot. **Tihelo** also has **injera** on the side.*

*The barley used for the dough is toasted before being milled. Known as **beso**, it is hard to buy outside Ethiopia. To make at home, toast pearl barley in a frying pan or in the oven and then grind in an electric spice or coffee grinder.*

SERVES 2–3

½ cup (3½ oz/100 g) pearl barley

salt

⅓ cup (80 ml) chilled buttermilk

1 garlic clove, mashed

1–2 pinches ground fenugreek

2 tablespoons plus 1 pinch *berbere* spice blend (page 40), or more to taste

3 tablespoons *tej* (page 10), or 3 tablespoons medium-dry white wine whisked with 1 teaspoon honey

1 tablespoon sunflower, canola, or other mild vegetable oil

8 oz (225 g) lean beef, such as top round or sirloin, cut into ½ inch (1.5 cm) cubes

1 tablespoon *niter kebbeh* (page 52) or clarified butter

Roast and grind the pearl barley following the instructions on page 205.

Sift three-quarters of the barley flour into a mixing bowl with a pinch of salt. With your fingertips, work in about 3 tablespoons of water until you have a thick dough. Place in a bowl and shape into a pointed cone, then set aside.

Make the *hazo* sauce. Whisk the buttermilk with 3 tablespoons of the reserved barley flour (you may have a small amount left over). Whisk in the garlic, fenugreek, and a pinch of *berbere*. Season with salt and set aside. (Traditionally, *helbet*, an intricate spice and grain flour blend, is used instead of barley flour to make *hazo*.)

Prepare the *tihelo* sauce. Place a saucepan over medium heat. Add the *tej* or the honey and wine mixture, along with the *berbere*, the remaining oil, and 1 cup (250 ml) of water. Simmer, uncovered, over medium heat for 10–15 minutes to round out the flavors and reduce to about ½ cup (125 ml). Generously season the meat with salt and add it to the pan. Cook for about 3 minutes until just done, then stir in the *niter kebbeh*.

Transfer the *tihelo* sauce to a serving bowl. Spoon some of the *hazo* sauce into the center (you can add more later) and serve with the barley dough on the side. To eat, make balls with pieces of dough and dip into the bowl.

አንጋ

Senga and the Kurt Culture

Ethiopia is home to one of the largest livestock populations in the African continent. With more than 100 million cattle, goats, and sheep combined,[1] they generate foreign currency through export, as well as satisfying our people's not-insignificant meat craving. Beef is most commonly eaten, mainly sourced from the humped zebu. This sub-species of domestic cattle came originally from India, and was introduced to Ethiopia around 1,500 BC via Somalia, by the Arabian Semetic people.[2] The cross-breeding between the humped zebu and taurine longhorns resulted in today's two most popular and dominant breeds, the Abyssinian and the Nilotic Sanga cattle.

While Christian fasting (see page 93) has brought diversification of our vegetarian recipes, meat remains important, with *kurt* as one of the fascinating and enduring Ethiopian food traditions. *Kurt*, the all-meat-platter, translates in Amharic to "a cut,"

referring to the manner in which meat is displayed to guests. With a minimum of 1 lb (450 g) to a maximum 11 lb (5 kg) per platter, *kurt* is an arrangement of different cuts of zebu accompanied with hot dipping sauce, *injera*, and sometimes breads. As it is one of the most popular dining options in the country, an average Ethiopian can consume 1 to 2 pounds (450 g to 1 kg) of *kurt* effortlessly, while famous restaurants like *Yilma*, *Ashu*, or *Misrake Bir* could get through five zebus within a day, especially for *Kebela* (the week before fasting begins). Some parts of the country, like Hossana and Konso, both south of Addis, would even have *kurt* as the preferred breakfast.

Artifacts in Axum are sufficient proof that Sanga cattle has been used for thousands of years to work the land, but the exact introduction of its consumption in raw form remains a mystery, even though it is associated with warfare.

Indeed, Ethiopia has seen multiple shifts of power, and regional rulers fought for the throne, even before the country converted to Judaism during the Solomonic Dynasty with Menelik I, in 950 BC.[3] During one of these battles, soldiers are said to have started eating raw meat to avoid attracting enemies via smoke and food aromas. The use of spicy and highly salted dipping mixes, both in dry and wet forms, were used to flavor the raw meat and also to preserve it over time.

Today, *kurt* has become an esteemed meal with local names[4]— Harar Sanga and Borena Sanga are famous breeds for instance, and each region has its own know-how and husbandry for breeding. Aging the beef is important in raw meat restaurants, also known as *Lookanda Bet* and *Kurt Bet*. Traditionally, aging

demands that the meat be on display a minimum of 24–48 hours on a stainless steel structure. Split in two along the spine, raw Sanga is exhibited and eaten in most Ethiopian cities, especially on Thursdays, Saturdays, and Sundays. Almost all parts of the zebu can be served raw, including the tongue, tripe, and liver. Make sure to request the best cuts, which are the *dabit*, the *shagna* (the hump), the *shent* (rib-eyes), among which the first cut-rib is called *sebrada* and the famous proverb goes: "*Sebrada, sebro wede guada, aysetem le bada*," which means "The first rib should be separated and reserved in the back room so you can take it out when someone dear visits."

1. International Trade Administration *Ethiopia—Livestock* (2017). Available at www.export.gov/article?id=Ethiopia-Livestock
2. J.E.O. Rege "The state of African Cattle genetic resources I. Classification framework and identification of threatened and extinct breeds" (1999) *International Livestock Research Institute (ILRI)*. Available at www.cattlenetwork.net/docs/agri/agri25_1.pdf

3. "The Ark of the Covenant: The Ethiopian Tradition." Retrieved 19/05/2010.
3. Domestic Animal Genetic Resources Information System (DAGRIS). Available at dagris.ilri.cgiar.org.

Buttery Spiced Raw Tenderloin

Gored-gored makes the third of the trio of famous Ethiopian raw beef dishes. While **kurt** (see page 140–41) comes in large hunks to cut yourself and dip into an assortment of piquant sauces, **gored-gored** is not only served in small, bite-size cubes, but also already bathed in melted **niter kebbeh** and spices. As with the other raw beef dishes, use only the choicest, freshest cuts bought from a reputable butcher.

SERVES 3–4

1 lb 2 oz (500 g) lean rib-eye, top round,
    or sirloin beef
salt
¼ cup (2 oz/60 g) *niter kebbeh* (page 52)
    or clarified butter
⅓ cup (80 ml) *awaze* dipping sauce (page 45)

Trim the fat and gristle from the meat. Cut into smallish bite-size cubes no larger than ¾ inch (2 cm) in size and season with salt.

In a saucepan, melt the *niter kebbeh* over low heat, add the *awaze*, and cook, stirring well, for 1 minute until well combined. Remove from the heat and leave to cool for a few minutes.

Place the meat in the saucepan and turn to coat evenly and thoroughly with the buttery chili sauce. Spoon into a serving bowl and serve immediately.

Beef Tripe and Tongue

This popular dish, cooked medium rare, is generally enjoyed for breakfast outside the fasting season (see page 93). The meat is usually raw, or at least rare, as the tongue and tripe lose their tenderness quite quickly once cooked. However, raw tripe can be hard to find in many places, as it is generally sold thoroughly cleaned and parboiled. This recipe for **melas sember** opts to cook it well done for those who are not used to eating tripe and tongue raw. The recipe also calls for parboiled tripe, but note that while it might come cooked, it still needs to be boiled for 1–2 hours to soften before adding to the pan with the tongue.

SERVES 4

8 oz (225 g) cleaned and parboiled beef tripe

8 oz (225 g) fresh veal tongue

2 tablespoons *niter kebbeh* (page 52)

mitmita spice blend (page 47)

salt

½ medium yellow onion, thinly sliced and separated

½ jalapeño pepper, seeded and sliced

Rinse the tripe thoroughly with plenty of cold running water. It should smell clean and fresh. Place in a large saucepan, cover with plenty of water, and boil for 1–2 hours until tender. Drain, trim into bite-size pieces, and set aside.

Using a sharp knife and your fingers, remove and discard the skin from the tongue. Trim away any gristle, fat, or tough sections, especially around the root end, then cut the meat into bite-size pieces.

In a large sauté pan, melt the *niter kebbeh* over high heat, add the tongue, season with *mitmita* and salt, and sauté for 30 seconds–1 minute. Add the tripe, onion, and jalapeño and cook, stirring continuously, for 1 minute. The tongue should be rare and the onion still crunchy. Serve hot.

Steak Tartar with Spiced Clarified Butter

*By far the most famous beef dish in Ethiopia is **kitfo**, finely minced beef blended with melted **niter kebbeh** and some **mitmita**. Although generally eaten raw (**tere**), it can be lightly cooked (**lebleb**) or even cooked (**yebesele**). Serve with collard greens or kale (see pages 80 and 42) and fresh cheese (see page 78).*

*A specific cut called **berundo** (within the round cut) is used for making **kitfo**. Since Ethiopian and western cuts are different, use only the freshest, highest-quality meat from a reputable source. Tell your butcher that you will be preparing it raw so he or she can give you the finest piece. Traditionally, the meat is patiently hand-chopped using a large knife, but it can also be ground, although connoissuers would feel the difference in texture.*

***Kitfo** originated in Guragé and while many Ethiopians eat it with **injera**, in this area **kocho**—"bread" made from the fermented pulp of the **enset** tree (see page 30)—is the preferred accompaniment. Traditionally, **kitfo** is served on an **enset** leaf (first toasted slightly to soften). Experts from the region also tend to look down upon the now-common practice of adding a pinch or two of freshly ground **korerima**, a local wild cardamom, to the **kitfo**.*

SERVES 4

1 lb 2 oz (500 g) lean rib-eye, top round, or
    sirloin beef

6 tablespoons (3½ oz/100 g) *niter kebbeh*
    (page 52)

mitmita spice blend (page 47)

salt

ground cardamom (optional)

Trim and discard the fat and gristle from the meat and then mince using a large, sharp chef's knife—it should be almost as fine as ground beef. Alternatively, have your butcher pass it twice through a meat grinder.

In a small saucepan, melt the *niter kebbeh* and set aside.

Place the meat in a large frying pan over low heat and quickly, without letting the meat brown, mix in the *niter kebbeh*, *mitmita*, and salt to taste. Add a pinch of cardamom, if desired. The meat should be warm but still raw. Serve with a bowl of *mitmita* on the side.

Raw Beef with Four Dipping Sauces

The tradition of eating raw meat is said to have come about as a consequence of soldiers not being allowed to light cooking fires at night (so as not to give away their location). The tradition then passed into the wider culture and remains strong today, especially on Thursdays, Saturdays, and Sundays outside of the fasting seasons (see page 93). Eating raw meat is also particularly associated with feasts that follow lengthy fasting periods. The ritual is that you slice off a generous-sized piece of meat for yourself with a knife and then dip it into one of an array of spicy sauces—see below. (Older generations of men like to hold the knife very close to their lips as they slice as a show of bravery.)

*Use only the freshest, highest-quality beef from a reputable butcher and serve with **tej**, beer, or a popular wine-based cocktail known as **awash tekesheno**, which blends together a dry white wine from the Awash winery, Bedele beer, and Sprite.*

SERVES 3–4

1 lb 2 oz (500 g) lean rib-eye, top round, or
   sirloin beef
homemade Ethiopian brown mustard (page 54)
awaze dipping sauce (page 45)
mitmita spice blend (page 47)
daata fresh chili dipping sauce (page 55)
injera (page 20)

Trim and discard the fat and gristle from the meat. Cut into large, 1 inch (2.5 cm) thick pieces and arrange on a serving plate.

Thin the mustard with hot water until runny and place in a small bowl. Spoon the other sauces and dips into individual bowls.

Cut the *injera* into strips about 3 inch (8 cm) long and roll. Serve alongside the meat.

Tenderloin with Coffee Sauce

Nowhere is coffee as present in daily life as in Ethiopia, where the beans are eaten as a snack (see page 9) as well as ground for the numerous cups of coffee that are consumed throughout the day. Roasted beans also make a very popular and interesting ingredient in the kitchen, and this recipe is a great example. Beef stock, infused with dark, roasted coffee beans, makes a simple but ideal sauce for tenderloin—delicious served with Creamy Scalloped Potatoes with Smoked Milk (see page 162).

SERVES 4–6

3¼ lb (1.5 kg) beef or veal bones

4 tablespoons olive oil

1 carrot, roughly chopped

2 celery stalks, roughly chopped

1 medium red or yellow onion, roughly chopped

salt

1 tablespoon tomato paste

1 fresh bouquet garni of thyme, bay leaf, and parsley, tied together

¼ cup (60 ml) red wine

½ cup (1¾ oz/50 g) whole dark roast coffee beans

1 lb 5 oz (600 g) beef tenderloin, cut into 4–6 pieces

Preheat the oven to 400°F (200°C).

Arrange the bones on a roasting pan and drizzle with 1 tablespoon of the oil. Roast for 45 minutes or so, turning from time to time until well browned.

Meanwhile, place a large stockpot over medium–high heat. Add 2 tablespoons of the oil and the carrot, celery, and onion. Season with salt and cook for 10 minutes, or until browned. Stir in the tomato paste. Transfer the bones to the stockpot along with the bouquet garni.

Pour the wine into the hot roasting pan to deglaze, stirring and scraping the base to release all the flavor. Transfer to the stockpot. Add 8½ cups (2 liters) of water to the pot and bring to a boil, then reduce the heat and gently simmer, uncovered, for 2–3 hours—the stock should have reduced to about 3 cups (700 ml). Add more water during this time if necessary. Strain, discarding all the solids.

Pour 2 cups (500 ml) of the hot stock into a saucepan and boil over high heat to reduce by about half or to your desired sauce consistency. In a separate saucepan, toast the roasted coffee beans until their aroma is released, add to the sauce, then remove from the heat and set aside to infuse for 5–10 minutes. Strain into a clean saucepan and set aside. (Refrigerate the remaining stock for up to one week or freeze to keep for longer.)

Season the meat with salt. Heat a heavy, cast-iron frying pan or ovensafe dish over high heat, add the remaining 1 tablespoon of oil, and sear the pieces of tenderloin on each side. Transfer the pan to the oven to finish cooking, turning once. When the meat is cooked to your liking, remove it from the oven and set aside to rest for 10 minutes while you reheat the sauce. Arrange the tenderloin on a serving plate and drizzle over the coffee sauce by straining and discarding the coffee beans. Serve with Creamy Scalloped Potatoes with Smoked Milk (see page 162), if you like.

Three-Meat Minced Lamb

*A classic breakfast dish using freshly butchered lamb, **dulet** is particularly popular for Easter. It is usually prepared medium rare, although here the dish is fully cooked. The key to a good **dulet** is in patiently chopping the ingredients very finely. If you can't find sheep tripe, use beef tripe instead.*

SERVES 4

9 oz (250 g) cleaned and parboiled sheep or beef tripe

9 oz (250 g) boneless lamb sirloin

5 oz (140 g) lamb liver

3½ tablespoons (1¾ oz/50 g) *niter kebbeh* (page 52) or clarified butter

½ medium red or yellow onion, finely chopped

2 garlic cloves, finely chopped

mitmita spice blend (page 47)

salt

1 tablespoon finely chopped jalapeño pepper

Rinse the tripe thoroughly with cold running water. It should smell clean and fresh. Place in a large saucepan, cover with plenty of water, and boil for 1–2 hours until tender. Drain. Trim into ¾ inch (2 cm) pieces and set aside.

Finely chop the tripe, sirloin, and liver, then mix together.

In a large sauté pan, melt the *niter kebbeh*, add the onion, and cook for 3–4 minutes over medium heat. Add the garlic and cook for about 1 minute until aromatic. Add the tripe, liver, and sirloin, and cook for 2–3 minutes, stirring continuously, until the liver just begins to lose its pinkness. Remove from the heat before it cooks completely. Season with *mitmita* and salt, stir in the jalapeño, and serve immediately.

Spicy Lamb Stew

*Slaughtering a lamb to celebrate a religious festivity, a birthday, or even a job promotion is common in Ethiopia. It takes place at home, with an expert brought in to help with the butchering. One of the popular dishes to prepare on such occasions is this spicy lamb stew, which traditionally uses pieces from both the front and rear legs of the animal. (Another dish is **dulet** (see page 149), finely chopped organ meat served medium-rare and eaten for breakfast while the rest of the animal is being butchered.)*

SERVES 4

1 bone-in leg of lamb (3–3½ lb/1.3–1.6 kg)

2 tablespoons sunflower, canola, or other mild vegetable oil

4 tablespoons *niter kebbeh* (page 52) or clarified butter

4 medium red or yellow onions, finely chopped (about 1 lb 2 oz/500 g)

1 tablespoon finely chopped garlic

1 tablespoon grated or finely chopped ginger

2 tablespoons *berbere* spice blend (page 40), or more to taste

1 teaspoon ground nigella seeds

salt

½ teaspoon *mekelesha* spice blend (page 44)

Have your butcher trim and debone the leg of lamb, reserving the bones. Cut the meat into generous 1 inch (3 cm) pieces. Use a cleaver to chop the bones into a few pieces. Set aside.

Place a heavy-bottomed sauté pan or wide saucepan over medium heat. Add the oil, 2 tablespoons of the *niter kebbeh*, and the onions, and cook for 10–15 minutes until soft and translucent. Stir in the garlic and ginger and cook for about 1 minute until aromatic. Stir in the *berbere* and the nigella with a couple of spoonfuls of water, cover, and cook over low heat for 10 minutes, stirring frequently. Add a touch of extra water if needed to keep it from scorching.

Season the meat with salt and add with the bones to the pan. Mix well and brown the meat for 5–10 minutes.

Add 1½ cups (350 ml) boiling water to the pan, stir again, and cover almost entirely with a lid. Cook for about 1½ hours until the lamb is tender and the sauce has thickened. Add a touch more water if it seems to be drying out or remove the lid completely to reduce the sauce if needed—it should not be overly runny.

Stir in the *mekelesha* and remaining 2 tablespoons of *niter kebbeh* and cook for a final 5 minutes. Serve, including the bone—traditionally the bone marrow of *Beg Siga Wat* is the most appreciated part of the meal.

Tender Lamb Cubes Simmered in a Mild Turmeric and Onion Sauce

*This dish is the mild sibling of **beg siga wat** (see page 151). However, though mild, it is not bland, since the turmeric and cumin-like spice ajowan, together with plenty of onion, garlic, and fresh ginger, give the dish its rich taste. Perfect for those who want flavor but not so much heat.*

SERVES 4–6

1 bone-in leg of lamb (3–3½ lb/1.3–1.6 kg)

3 tablespoons sunflower, canola, or other mild vegetable oil

4 tablespoons *niter kebbeh* (page 52) or clarified butter

4 medium red or yellow onions, finely chopped (about 1 lb 2 oz/500 g)

2 tablespoons finely chopped garlic

1 tablespoon grated or finely chopped fresh ginger

½ teaspoon ground turmeric

½ teaspoon ground ajowan

salt

2–3 medium jalapeño peppers, seeded and chopped, to garnish

Have your butcher trim and debone the leg of lamb, reserving the bones. Cut the meat into generous 1 inch (3 cm) pieces. Use a cleaver to chop the bones into a few pieces. Set aside.

Place a heavy-bottomed sauté pan or wide saucepan over medium heat. Add the oil and 2 tablespoons of the *niter kebbeh* and cook the onions for 10–15 minutes until soft and translucent. Stir in the garlic and ginger and cook for about 1 minute until aromatic. Stir in the turmeric and ajowan.

Season the meat with salt and add it, along with the bones. Mix well and brown the meat for about 5 minutes.

Add 2 cups (500 ml) of boiling water to the pan, cover almost entirely with a lid, and cook over low heat for about 1½ hours until the meat is tender and the sauce has reduced. Remove and discard the bones and stir in the remaining 2 tablespoons of *niter kebbeh*. Place in a serving bowl, garnish with the jalapeños, and serve.

Goat in Mild Turmeric Stew with Carrots

Goat and lamb stews in Ethiopia usually start with a base of slow-cooked onions (the **kulet**), *to which the meat gets added and allowed to slowly stew. This recipe, however, uses a slightly different method, as the name of the dish indicates—* **kikil** *means "boiled" in Amharic. However, the outcome is similar, which is to say, delicious.*

The key to a good stew is using plenty of bones and as much fat as possible. This gives taste and body to the stew. Buying goat bones separately can be difficult, so it's easiest to buy a large, bone-in leg. Have your butcher remove and cut the bones into pieces for you. Otherwise, use beef bones, which are more readily available.

SERVES 4

2 kid goat legs (about 1 lb/450 g each)

4 medium red or yellow onions, sliced
  (about 1 lb 2 oz/500 g)

3 medium carrots, peeled and cut crossways
  into 3 pieces

1 tablespoon finely chopped garlic

½ tablespoon grated or finely chopped ginger

½ teaspoon ground turmeric

½ teaspoon ajowan

2 tablespoons *niter kebbeh* (page 52) or
  clarified butter

salt

2 jalapeño peppers, cut in half and seeded

Injera (page 20), to serve

Have your butcher trim and debone the goat legs, reserving the bones. Cut the meat into generous 1 inch (3 cm) pieces. Use a cleaver to chop each bone into 2–3 pieces and set aside.

Place the meat and bones in a large saucepan, cover with about 8½ cups (2 liters) of water, and bring to a boil. Skim off the foam. Add the onions, carrots, garlic, ginger, turmeric, ajowan, and 1 tablespoon of the *niter kebbeh*, and season with salt.

Partly cover the pan and cook over low heat for 1½ hours, or until the meat is tender and the sauce has somewhat reduced. Add a touch more water if needed or remove the lid to reduce further if needed—the sauce should be thick and stewy.

Stir in the remaining 1 tablespoon of *niter kebbeh* and add the jalapeños. Roll up pieces of *injera*, tuck them into the sides to soak up the sauce, and serve straight from the pan.

Cabbage Rolls with Lamb Tongue

Cabbage—probably the favorite vegetable in Ethiopia—combines perfectly with one of our country's beloved delicacies, lamb tongue, and in no better manner than as these cabbage rolls. Net-like caul fat, or lace fat, shown in the image uncooked, is the fatty netting that surrounds the internal organs of some animals such as lambs or cows. It is available from specialist butchers. The rolls will be golden brown once cooked.

Clean the tongues thoroughly in plenty of cold running water. Bring a large pot of water to a boil, season with salt, and add the tongues. Cover the pot and gently simmer for about 1½ hours until tender. Remove the tongues and set aside to cool. If desired, peel away the white skin.

Generously dust the tongues with ajowan and cumin. Roll each tongue in a slice of bacon and secure with a toothpick. In a sauté pan over medium heat, add 1 tablespoon of the oil and cook the rolled tongues for 3–4 minutes until the bacon is crispy, turning as needed. Transfer to paper towels to drain and remove the toothpicks.

Remove 12 large leaves from the cabbage. If necessary, trim the thick bottom stem. Bring a wide, deep pan of salted water to a boil, add a couple of leaves at a time, and boil for 2–3 minutes until tender. Transfer with a slotted spoon to paper towels to dry, then flatten each leaf with a rolling pin.

Take a flattened cabbage leaf and place a bacon-wrapped tongue at the bottom edge. Roll the leaf around the tongue, tucking in the sides. Then place this package on a second flattened leaf and roll in the same manner. Finally, place this on top of a piece of caul and snugly roll. Repeat with the remaining tongues.

Preheat the oven to 350°F (180°C).

In a large frying pan, add the remaining 1 tablespoon of oil over medium heat and lightly sear the cabbage rolls for about 1 minute on each side. Pour in the stock and simmer for about 5 minutes, basting regularly. Transfer the rolls to a baking dish, drizzle over the cooking juices from the pan, and bake, basting frequently, for 20–30 minutes until heated through. Reserve the sauce.

To serve, cut the rolls in half and drizzle the sauce over them.

MAKES 6 ROLLS

6 fresh lamb tongues, each 3–4 oz (80–115 g)
salt
ground ajowan, for dusting
ground cumin, for dusting
6 slices kosher (beef) bacon
2 tablespoons olive oil
1 head of savoy cabbage, cored
6 cubes of sheep caul fat, each about 6 inches (15 cm)
⅓ cup (80 ml) chicken stock

የበግ እንፍሌ | BEG ENFELE

Festive Dipped Leg of Lamb

This rather theatrical dish was once standard at great feasts. Trimmed in a special way, a leg of lamb would briefly simmer in a spicy sauce and then be hoisted out of the pot, and have pieces trimmed off to serve to guests. The leg then went back into the pot to cook for a little longer before being pulled back out, with more pieces trimmed and served, and so on.

*Preparing **beg enfele** in the kitchen is surprisingly easy and doesn't even require a very large pot (in fact, a medium-size one is preferable in order to submerge the meat deeply in the sauce). The main work involved is in the **zilzil** process—the unique method of cutting the leg of lamb without fully detaching it from the bone. First, the upper bone—correctly called the leg bone (the lower one is the shank)—must be removed, while the shank stays in place. From this heavy, top section of boneless meat, a succession of cuts should create long strips of meat that remain attached to the leg.*

*The dish can be prepared in advance up to the actual cooking of the meat. Simply remove the pot from the heat, cover, and bring back to a low boil when you are ready. When you trim the pieces of meat, catch the delicious drips in the pot or over **injera**, which will soak it up nicely. Be warned—the sauce is quite heavily spiced to ensure the meat is packed with flavor during the short cooking time.*

SERVES 4–8

generous ¼ cup (1 oz/30 g) *berbere* spice blend
    (page 40)
2 cups (500 ml) *tej* (page 10), or medium-dry
    white wine whisked with 3 tablespoons honey
1 bone-in leg of lamb (1.3–1.6 kg)
salt and freshly ground black pepper
1 tablespoon sunflower, canola, or other mild
    vegetable oil
2 tablespoons *niter kebbeh* (page 52) or
    clarified butter
4 medium red or yellow onions, finely chopped
    (about 1 lb 2 oz/500 g)
1½ tablespoons finely chopped garlic
1½ tablespoons grated or finely chopped ginger
1 teaspoon ground cardamom
1 tablespoon ground ajowan
1 lb 2 oz (500 g) beef bones

In a small bowl, make a paste with the *berbere* and 2½ tablespoons of the *tej*. Set aside to allow the spice to mellow slightly.

Trim and discard any fat from around the leg of lamb. Remove the leg bone (the upper one), or ask your butcher to do it. Along the inside of the leg, follow the leg bone with a sharp knife, cutting the meat away to free it. Carefully cut at the knee joint between the leg and shank bones; pull away the leg bone. Use a cleaver to chop the bone into a couple of pieces then set aside.

In the boneless top part of the leg, cut *zilzil* strips. Begin by making two parallel cuts about ¾ inch (2 cm) apart, as far as possible into the thickest part of the leg. With the blade at the end of one, cut about three-quarters of the way across the top towards the other and then down, in an inverted L shape, unfurling the piece rather than detaching it. Make another two or three L-shaped cuts to create a strip 7–12 inches (18–30 cm) in length (see pages 158–9). Cut the remaining leg into *zilzil* strips. Season generously with salt and black pepper and set aside.

In a large sauté pan over medium heat, combine the oil and 1 tablespoon of *niter kebbeh* and cook the onions for 5–10 minutes until softened. Add the garlic and ginger and cook for about 1 minute until aromatic. Stir in the reserved *berbere* paste, the cardamom, and ajowan, and cook for 5 minutes, adding a spoonful of water if needed to completely blend the seasonings.

Pour in 1 cup (250 ml) of the *tej* and cook for about 5 minutes, stirring frequently, until it has largely evaporated. Pour in the remaining scant 1 cup (210 ml) of *tej* and cook for about 10 minutes until it has reduced down. Add the reserved lamb and beef bones.

Add 10½ cups (2.5 liters) of boiling water to the pot and let the sauce simmer, uncovered, for 1 hour, stirring frequently. Skim off any foam that forms on the surface. You should be left with about 4¼ cups (1 liter) of sauce at the end—add some boiling water if needed. Stir in the remaining 1 tablespoon of *niter kebbeh*.

Firmly holding the leg by the (foot) end, submerge the trimmed pieces into the sauce and cook until the ends are medium rare, about 5 minutes. While another person carefully holds the leg above the pot, grasp the end of a strip with tongs and trim away pieces about 3–4 inches (8–10 cm) long using kitchen scissors. Return the leg to the sauce to continue cooking. Serve the cut pieces immediately.

Lift the leg up out of the sauce and trim as pieces become done, gradually cooking and cutting away all of the meat.

Smoked Milk or Water

There are two species of olive trees in Ethiopia: the East African olive, and the African wild olive, both with tall, dense crowns, white flowers, and strong, durable wood used for making tools and furniture. People also use the wood for smoking water or milk, a popular tradition in Ethiopia that adds flavor and assists in preserving the milk in places without refrigeration. If you can't find olive wood, strip the needles off a dry branch of rosemary and use that instead. The flavor is different but pleasing.

If using a small jug, a single twig of olive wood should give off enough smoke to flavor the liquid. For 8 ½ cups (2 liters) use a couple of twigs, and for larger quantities, four or five of them. Add a sprig of fresh or dried rue to the pot for a bitter touch. Water can be kept, and will retain its flavor, for about a week. Store smoked milk in the refrigerator for two days.

MAKES 8½ CUPS (2 LITERS)

2–4 small olive wood twigs or smoking chips
8½ cups (2 liters) milk or fresh water

You will need a tall clay pot or jug, preferably with a mouth that is narrower than the base. An old-fashioned stoneware bean pot will work, as will a lidded pickle crock.

Wash the pot out with fresh, room-temperature water. Do not dry out the inside. Place upside down to drain, but do not let it fully dry.

Light one end of the twigs until a flame is burning. Blow out and immediately place under the inverted pot so that the smoke fills the container for 30–60 seconds, depending on the size of the container.

In one quick motion, in order to avoid letting too much of the smoke escape, turn the pot over, fill with milk (or water), and tightly cover with a lid. To ensure that no smoke escapes, use foil or plastic wrap to seal the edges of the lid.

Store water in a dry, cool place for up to one week. Store milk in the refrigerator for two days.

Creamy Scalloped Potatoes with Smoked Milk

The tradition of smoking milk with fresh rue is said to help keep it fresh in places without refrigeration. However, it also creates plenty of flavor and so brings an original twist to classic dishes like these scalloped potatoes. The potatoes go particularly well with bold meat dishes, such as Tenderloin with Coffee Sauce (see page 148) or a rack of lamb.

SERVES 6

2¼ lb (1 kg) medium waxy potatoes, peeled and cut crossways into ⅛ inch (3 mm) slices

4¼ cups (1 liter) smoked milk (page 160), at room temperature

½ whole nutmeg, freshly grated

salt and freshly ground black pepper

Preheat the oven to 400°F (200°C).

In a large saucepan, combine the potatoes and smoked milk and bring to a boil. Reduce the heat and simmer for about 10 minutes until the potatoes are just tender. Using a slotted spoon, transfer the potatoes to a casserole or gratin dish.

Continue simmering the milk over medium heat until it has reduced to a generous 1½ cups (375 ml). Season with nutmeg, salt, and black pepper, then pour the milk mixture over the potatoes.

Bake, uncovered, for about 20 minutes until golden and creamy. Serve.

Afar Roasted Leg of Kid Goat with Yellow Rice

This recipe comes from the arid, far northeastern area of Afar, a very hot region of traditionally nomadic pastoralists. The dish is cooked in ovens dug into the ground. Hot coals are placed in the bottom of a hole and the goat leg is then suspended on a pole (threaded through the tendon) and dangled above the embers, and the hole is covered with a lid. Of course it's a little hard to reproduce this exactly at home, so we've provided instructions for cooking in a home oven. If you don't have a roasting rack, suspend the legs in a deep pan using stainless steel iron sticks. The goal is to keep the goat legs off the bottom of the pan.

"Bekel" refers to a young goat, and in Afar a young goat can range from 15 days to three months old. The younger the goat, the more esteemed the guest the dish is prepared for. Use the legs of kid goats, which weigh about 1 lb (450 g) each. Cooks in Afar also prepare a lovely range of rice dishes, including a spiced, turmeric-yellow one that goes perfectly with this roasted goat (recipe is given below).

SERVES 4

2 generous tablespoons ground cumin
cayenne pepper
freshly ground black pepper
salt
2 kid goat legs (about 1 lb/450 g each)
sunflower, canola, or other light
   vegetable oil, for coating

For turmeric rice

2 cups (14 oz/400 g) basmati rice
1 tablespoon sunflower, canola, or other
   mild vegetable oil
½ medium red or yellow onion, finely chopped
¼ teaspoon ground cumin
¼ teaspoon ground turmeric
2 teaspoons fresh lemon juice

Preheat the oven to 350°F (180°C).

In bowl, blend the cumin with cayenne, black pepper, and salt. Rub the goat legs with oil and a generous amount of the spice blend so that the meat is coated all over.

Arrange the legs on the rack of a large roasting pan. Drizzle about ½ cup (125 ml) of water into the bottom. Cover the pan snugly with foil and place in the oven. After 40 minutes, turn the legs, add more water to the pan if needed, and replace the foil snugly. Cook for a final 20–30 minutes or until the legs are tender. Remove the foil for the last 5 or so minutes of cooking time to brown the meat.

Remove from the oven, remove the bones, and serve with the rice.

To cook turmeric rice

Wash the rice in various changes of cold water until it runs almost clear. Place in a bowl, cover with water, and leave to soak for 30 minutes. Drain.

In a wide saucepan, heat the oil over medium heat, add the onion, and cook for about 8 minutes until slightly browned. Stir in the cumin and turmeric, add the rice, stir to blend well, and cook for a further minute.

Add 2¼ cups (1 liter) of boiling water to the rice and stir well. Reduce the heat to low, cover the pan, and cook for about 15 minutes until the rice is tender. Remove the pan from the heat and leave, covered, for 5–10 minutes without lifting the lid.

Drizzle the lemon juice over the rice, toss, and serve.

Lamb-Stuffed Vegetables

*Doro effeta is the excess oil that rises to the top of the stew when preparing **doro wat** (see page 170), our country's most celebrated dish. The spicy heat congregates here and so whoever is serving gently pushes it to the side when dishing up. However, it shouldn't go to waste, since it can be used as a seasoning in a variety of dishes. If you don't have any **doro effeta**, substitute with **niter kebbeh** (see page 52) mixed with a few generous pinches of **berbere** spice blend (see page 40). This recipe calls for ground lamb, but the shredded meat from a roasted leg of goat would be even better.*

SERVES 4–6

2 red peppers

2 large waxy potatoes

2 large red onions, peeled

2 large zucchinis

salt

2 teaspoons sunflower, canola, or other
   mild vegetable oil, plus extra for
   greasing the pan

1 garlic clove, finely chopped

1 lb (450 g) ground lamb

freshly ground black pepper

2 ripe tomatoes, peeled and finely chopped

4 tablespoons *doro effeta* (oil from cooking
   doro wat, see above)

1 cup (250 ml) chicken stock

4 tablespoons (2 oz/60 g) butter,
   cut into pieces

Wash the peppers, potatoes, and onions and trim the bottoms of each so that they will sit flat, then cut off a top section too to act as a cap. Peel the zucchinis in stripes, trim the ends, and cut them in half crossways. Hollow out the inside of the vegetables and set aside, reserving the inside parts. Finely chop the latter with a sharp knife or in a food processor.

In a large saucepan of salted water, boil the potatoes for about 15 minutes until just tender. Drain and set aside.

In a large sauté pan over medium heat, add the oil, garlic, and lamb, season with salt and black pepper, and cook for 3–5 minutes until just browned. Add the reserved chopped vegetables and the tomatoes and cook, stirring frequently, for about 10 minutes until the vegetables have lost their rawness. Transfer to a mixing bowl and stir in 2 tablespoons of the *doro efetta*.

Preheat the oven to 400°F (200°C).

Fill the vegetable shells with the stuffing, packing it in tightly. Arrange in a baking dish and cover with the caps. Pour the stock around the base and dot with pieces of butter. Cover with foil and bake for 30–45 minutes, basting from time to time, until the vegetables are somewhat tinender and well coated with the sticky sauce. Drizzle the remaining 2 tablespoons of *doro effeta* over the vegetables and serve.

7

Poultry, Eggs & Fish

Slow-Cooked Spicy Chicken with Hard-Boiled Eggs

Ethiopia's most famous dish is the queen of the festive table—and almost always made in feast-size quantities, generally using a whole chicken, a dozen eggs, and many kilos of onions. This recipe calls for four pieces of chicken and four eggs and so allows for a piece of meat and an egg for each person, plus plenty of sauce. Feel free to add another drumstick or two to the pot, but remember this is a dish largely about the sauce, so try to resist the temptation to overwhelm it with too much meat.

*The onions should be very finely chopped. They give the final sauce its body and texture, so use a food processor if possible. Here, they are cooked in the traditional manner, which means they are sweated first without any oil or **niter kebbeh**. However, you can add the oil with the onion at the beginning, if desired.*

SERVES 4

2 whole free-range chicken legs

1 lime or small lemon, cut in half

6 tablespoons (1½ oz/40 g) *berbere* spice blend (page 40)

4 medium red or yellow onions, very finely chopped (about 1 lb 2 oz/500 g)

3 tablespoons sunflower, canola, or other mild vegetable oil

3 tablespoons *niter kebbeh* (page 52) or clarified butter, or more to taste

1 heaped tablespoon finely chopped garlic

½ tablespoon grated or finely chopped ginger

a pinch of ground nigella seeds

a pinch of ground cardamom

a tiny pinch of ground ajowan

salt

½ teaspoon *mekelesha* spice blend (page 44)

4 eggs, hard-boiled and peeled

injera (page 20), to serve

Remove the skin from the chicken legs and split each leg at the joint into drumsticks and thighs. Rinse well and then place in a bowl of cold water with the lime to soak.

In a small bowl, make a thick paste by blending the *berbere* with about 2½ tablespoons of water. Set aside to allow the spices to mellow slightly.

In a heavy-bottomed sauté pan, cook the onion over medium–low heat, stirring very frequently, for about 15 minutes until soft and translucent. Stir in the oil and 2 tablespoons of the *niter kebbeh*, add the garlic and ginger, and cook for about 1 minute until aromatic. Stir in the reserved *berbere* paste, the nigella, cardamom, and ajowan, and season with salt. Add a couple of spoonfuls of water and cook over a low heat for 10 minutes, stirring frequently, to let the aromas smooth out. Add a touch more water if needed to keep the mixture from scorching.

Drain the chicken and gently squeeze to remove any moisture. With a sharp knife, mark the pieces on each side with a pair of diagonal shallow slits. Add the chicken to the pan, coating in the sauce, and cook for about 5 minutes until browned. Add 1 cup (250 ml) of hot water, cover the pot, and simmer for about 15 minutes until the chicken is almost tender. Transfer the chicken to a plate and cover.

Cover the pan with a lid and simmer the sauce over low heat for 1 hour. Add the *mekelesha* spice blend and cook for a further 15 minutes. Add more water if needed to keep the consistency moist. Return the chicken to the pan to reheat. Make shallow slits horizontally on the boiled eggs and add to the stew. Serve with *injera*.

Tej

Gondar sits in the foothills of the Simien Mountains at a crossroads of two important ancient trade routes that cross the north of the country.[1] Founded in 1635 by Emperor Fasilides, it served as imperial capital for 250 years. Ruins of castle-like palaces, once home to emperors, kings, and courtiers, hint at its past glory.

One legacy of that era is its reputation for *tej*, fermented honey wine or mead, once the drink of the ruling class (commoners drank *tella*, home-brewed beer).

Tej today is enormously popular in Ethiopia across all social lines. Ethiopia is Africa's largest producer of honey and the ninth largest in the world.[2] A staggering 80 percent of that considerable honey production goes into making *tej*.[3]

There are few commercial brands of the drink, though. People generally buy refilled containers of it from a neighborhood *tej bet*—literally "tej house"—from raw meat restaurants such as *Lukanda Bet*, or even brew it themselves.

It takes four or five weeks to make a batch of *tej* using raw honey, water, and some *gesho*, a shrubby local species of buckthorn that causes the brew to ferment. As it ferments in a covered bucket, yeast forms and converts the sugars in the concoction into alcohol. Filtered into bottles and served in small *berele*, bulbous, narrow-necked flasks, the cloudy-gold brew tastes simultaneously sweet and pungent. After an initial sourness comes a lingering sweetness that, when well made, contains hints of honey-ripe apricots and peaches.

While an in-depth study of *tej* samples across the country found the alcohol content fluctuating widely between 2.7 and a knee-buckling 21.7 percent, the mean value stands between 7 and 11 percent[4] (beer is roughly 5 percent). Thus 1 or 2 cups can easily get you dizzy, especially if using *berele* to drink it. The flask is intentionally shaped to avoid losing alcohol through air dissipation and made specifically to forgo all hints consumers could gain from smelling it and realizing its effect. Thus, if tasting *tej* in *berele* for the first time, make sure to stand up every once in a while to check if you're feeling too

dizzy to walk. A less potent version called *berz* is popular, too. The honey and water mixture is not allowed to ferment long enough to develop much, or even any, alcohol content.

In Gondar, the most famous *tej bet* is the long-running Abekelesh, named for the current proprietor's grandmother and immortalized in a popular song:

> *There's laughter, there's games, and fame in the house,*
> *I really love the house of Abekelesh.*

As in other *tej bets* in the city, the favorite accompaniment to the drink is *bekolt*, small brown fava beans that have been sprouted, boiled, and then tossed in a generous blend of runny, nose-pinching mustard and chili sauce. "When we eat this, we feel less drunk," said one Abekelesh customer. He sat with a

dozen other men at a table topped with an equal number of *bereles* of *tej* glowing brilliant gold in the light of the open door. "Also, because it is spicy, we appreciate the sweet flavors of the drink more."

The song compares Abekelesh, the past owner, to the queen of Gondar, a deeply favorable association. But then, in the following line, it changes tone:

> *She is finishing all the youngsters' money with her tej.*

By the number of clients in Abekelesh today, and the number of bottles of *tej* they consume, the song retains some truth. The *tej* is certainly as good, or at least as potent, as the original Abekelesh's, even if many of the customers could no longer be described as young.

---

1. Bahru Zewde *A History of Modern Ethiopia* (Ohio University Press) p.21.
2. http://ethioagp.org/honey-2/
3. http://ethioagp.org/honey-2/
4. World Health Organisation *Global Status Report on Alcohol 2004* (2004). Available at www.who.int/substance_abuse/publications/en/ethiopia.pdf

Chicken in Tej Sauce with Oranges

*Along with **tella** (the traditional beer), **tej** is our country's iconic tipple, but it can also be used as an ingredient. This modern recipe uses the fermented honey wine to make a glazy sauce, with the orange segments providing hints of citric freshness. Serve with puréed turnips.*

Preheat the oven to 400°F (200°C).

Season the chicken inside with salt and black pepper and stuff with the thyme and parsley. Truss the chicken by tying the legs together with kitchen string and rub the outside skin with the oil. Blend the *berbere* with salt and black pepper and sprinkle all over the outside of the bird.

Grease a large cast-iron roasting dish or pan with oil and place the chicken on it breast-side down. Arrange the carrot, celery, and onion around the bird and cover with foil. Roast for about 30 minutes, then turn the chicken breast-side up and cover with the foil. Add a splash of water if the vegetables threaten to burn and roast for a further 30 minutes until the juices run clear and a thermometer inserted into the thickest part of the thigh reads 170°F (75°C). Remove the foil and continue to cook until the skin turns golden.

SERVES 4–6

1 whole chicken (4½–5 lb/2–2.3kg)
salt and freshly ground black pepper
a small handful of fresh thyme sprigs
a small handful of fresh flat-leaf parsley sprigs
1 tablespoon olive oil, plus more for greasing
½ tablespoon *berbere* spice blend (page 40), for seasoning
1 medium carrot, roughly chopped
1 celery stalk, roughly chopped
1 medium red or yellow onion, roughly chopped
2 ripe medium oranges
1 cup (250 ml) *tej* (page 10), or medium-dry white wine whisked with 1 tablespoon honey
¼ cup (60 ml) heavy cream

Carefully transfer the chicken to a chopping board, cut away the string, and remove and discard the herbs. Cover the chicken in foil and let it rest for 15 minutes.

Meanwhile, using a sharp knife, peel the oranges and trim away the white pith. Working over a bowl to catch any juices, carefully cut along the membranes and remove the individual segments. Set aside with the juices.

While the chicken is resting, pour the *tej* into the hot roasting pan to deglaze, stirring and scraping to release all the flavor, and cook on the stovetop for about 1 minute, stirring. Stir in the cream and simmer gently until the sauce thickens. Strain the sauce into a bowl, pressing out all the juices from the vegetables using the back of a ladle. Discard the vegetables. Season the sauce with salt and pepper to taste and add the orange segments and reserved juices.

Carve the chicken and serve with a drizzle of sauce and some orange segments spooned over the top.

Chicken Simmered in a Mild Onion and Turmeric Sauce

If **doro wat** is the queen of the festive table, then one of her consorts is the aromatic, golden **doro alicha**. Rather than **berbere** doing the heavy lifting on spice, the turmeric and cumin give an earthiness to the copious, sweet onion that fills the sauce. It is a perfect option for those who prefer less piquant dishes but love full-bodied flavors.

As with **doro wat**, onions are key to the dish—use plenty and be patient in finely chopping them, or chop in a food processor. Adding more **niter kebbeh** will give it a silkier final texture and more flavor, and don't forget to slip some peeled hard-boiled eggs into the sauce before serving, to give the dish a festive touch.

SERVES 4

3 tablespoons sunflower, canola, or other mild vegetable oil

4 medium red or yellow onions, finely chopped

2 tablespoons finely chopped garlic

1 tablespoon grated or finely chopped ginger

3 tablespoons *niter kebbeh* (page 52) or clarified butter, or more to taste

½ teaspoon ground turmeric

¼ teaspoon ground cumin

salt

8 skinless chicken drumsticks

hard-boiled eggs, to serve

injera (page 20) or bread, to serve

In a large sauté pan or wide saucepan, add the oil and cook the onions over medium heat for 10–15 minutes until soft and translucent. Add the garlic and ginger and cook for about 1 minute until aromatic. Stir in 2 tablespoons of the *niter kebbeh*, and the turmeric and cumin, and season with salt. Cover and cook over low heat for 10 minutes to round out the flavors. Add a touch of water if necessary to keep the mixture from scorching.

Add the chicken, turn to coat, and cook uncovered for about 8 minutes until browned. Add 1½ cups (350 ml) of hot water, partly cover, and simmer over low heat for about 30 minutes until the chicken is tender.

Transfer the chicken to a plate. Increase the heat and reduce the sauce for about 5 minutes, so that it is saucy but not watery. Stir in the remaining *niter kebbeh*, return the chicken to the pot, and turn the drumsticks gently to coat. Using a sharp knife, make horizontal slits in the eggs and add them to the stew, then serve with *injera* or bread.

Buttermilk-Marinated Chicken with Grilled Vegetables

Soaking chicken in buttermilk helps tenderize the meat, and the spices in the marinade bring some lovely flavor to the finished dish.

SERVES 6

1½ cups (350 ml) plus 2 tablespoons buttermilk

1 teaspoon ground cardamom

½ tablespoon *berbere* spice blend (page 40)

6 whole chicken legs, split at the joint into drumsticks and thighs

3 small eggplants, cut in half lengthways

5 tablespoons sunflower oil

1 zucchini, peeled and cut crossways into ½ inch (1 cm) thick pieces

3 ripe medium tomatoes, cut in half

1½ cups (350 ml) stock

1 teaspoon ground turmeric

½ tablespoon *niter kebbeh* (page 52) or clarified butter

salt

In a large bowl, mix together 1½ cups (350 ml) of the buttermilk with the cardamom and *berbere* and submerge the chicken pieces in the marinade. Place in the refrigerator to marinate for 1 hour.

Preheat the oven to 425°F (220°C).

Heat a griddle pan over high heat, lightly brush the eggplant with 2 tablespoons of the oil, and cook, cut-side down, for about 5 minutes on each side until nicely seared. Remove, carefully wrap in foil, and cook in the oven for 30–40 minutes until tender. Remove from the oven and set aside. Do not remove the foil wrapping.

Brush the zucchini and tomatoes lightly with 1 tablespoon of the oil, and griddle in the same pan for 3–5 minutes per side. Cover to keep warm and set aside.

Remove the chicken from the buttermilk marinade, pat dry with paper towels, and discard the marinade. In a large sauté pan, heat the remaining 2 tablespoons of oil over medium heat and cook the chicken pieces for about 30 minutes until done. Add the stock, turmeric, and *niter kebbeh*, season with salt, and cook for a few minutes, basting the chicken.

Transfer the chicken to a serving dish and keep warm. Stir the remaining 2 tablespoons of buttermilk into the sauce and cook until it has slightly thickened. Pour the sauce over the chicken and serve with the grilled vegetables.

Nigella-Glazed Roast Chicken and Black and White Sesame Seeds

*While nigella is commonly used as a spicing ingredient in **niter kebbeh** (see page 52), in our cuisine its primary use is to flavor Ethiopian traditional baked breads. Nigella produces a fresh and rich flavor when roasted, which is precisely what is sought in this whole chicken recipe. This glazed chicken exploits the properties of some of our cuisine's key spices in a delicious combination of sesame and nigella.*

SERVES 4–6

1 small whole chicken (3–4 lb/1.4–1.8 kg)

1 teaspoon salt

1 teaspoon freshly ground black pepper

1 small bunch each of fresh thyme, parsley, and oregano

2 tablespoons sunflower, canola, or other mild vegetable oil, plus extra for oiling

3 tablespoons ground nigella seeds

1 medium red or yellow onion, halved

2 medium carrots, peeled and cut in half lengthways, then crossways

2¼ lb (1 kg) small waxy potatoes, rinsed

2 cups (500 ml) chicken stock

1 tablespoon butter

2 tablespoons sesame seeds (a mix of black and white if possible)

Preheat the oven to 425°F (220°C).

Season the inside of the chicken with half of the salt and black pepper, stuff with the fresh herbs, and truss the chicken by tying the legs together with kitchen string. Rub the skin with 1 tablespoon of the oil, the nigella, and remaining salt and pepper.

Grease a roasting pan with oil. Place the chicken breast-side down in the pan and roast for 15 minutes, just enough to brown the skin lightly. Reduce the oven temperature to 400°F (200°C). In a bowl, toss the onion, carrots, and potatoes with the remaining 1 tablespoon of oil. In a saucepan, bring the chicken stock to a simmer, cover, and keep hot.

Turn the chicken breast-side up. Arrange the onion, carrots, and potatoes around the bird, pour the stock over the vegetables, and cover the pan with foil. Bake for about 45 minutes until the chicken juices run clear and a thermometer inserted into the thickest part of the thigh reads 170°F (75°C).

Carefully transfer the chicken to a chopping board and pour all the juices from the pan into a 10–12 inch (25–30 cm) cast-iron ovensafe pan. Cut away the string from the bird and remove and discard the herbs. If the vegetables are cooked, simply cover to keep warm; if they are not yet fork-tender, cover with foil and return the pan to the oven to finish cooking.

Preheat the broiler. Place the cast-iron pan containing the meat juices over medium heat and add the butter. When melted, set the chicken in the pan breast-side up and baste until glossy, then sprinkle the sesame seeds all over the top.

Place the chicken under the broiler for about 5 minutes until the seeds are lightly toasted. Remove from the oven and let the chicken rest for about 15 minutes before carving. Pour the sauce from the pan into a bowl. Serve the chicken with the vegetables and the sauce on the side.

Creamy Chicken and Sweet Potatoes with Stuffed Green Chilies

*On our traditional table, chicken is synonymous with the festive favorite **doro wat** (see page 170). Here, however, it is given a modern twist and cooked in a creamy sauce that pairs perfectly with stuffed chilies, **senig** (see page 97).*

SERVES 4–6

4 bone-in whole chicken legs (drumsticks and thighs) with skin (about 2 lb 10 oz/1.2 kg)

1 tablespoon sunflower, canola, or other mild vegetable oil

2 medium carrots, roughly chopped

1 medium yellow or red onion, roughly chopped

2 celery stalks, roughly chopped

salt

1 bouquet garni of rosemary, thyme, and parsley, tied together

2 medium sweet potatoes, peeled and quartered lengthways

5 tablespoons (2½ oz/70 g) butter

8 oz (225 g) oyster or sliced button mushrooms

4–6 Mexican Anaheim chilies or another long, thin green chili peppers

¼ cup (1 oz/30 g) all-purpose flour

Place the chicken in a large saucepan, cover with water, and bring to a boil. Reduce the heat a little and simmer for 30–40 minutes until tender, then remove from the heat and set aside to cool. Remove and discard the skin, debone, pick out the meat in large pieces and reserve the bones. Cover the meat and set aside.

In a large saucepan over medium heat, add the oil, carrots, onion, and celery, season with salt, and cook for about 5 minutes until fragrant. Add the bouquet garni, reserved chicken bones, and 4¼ cups (1 liter) of water and bring to a boil, then reduce the heat. Cover the pot and simmer for 15 minutes. Add the sweet potatoes and simmer for about 15 minutes until tender, then remove with a slotted spoon and reserve. Strain the stock—you will have about 3 cups (700 ml)—and spoon out the carrots and reserve. Discard the remaining solids.

In a sauté pan, melt 1 tablespoon of the butter over medium heat, add the mushrooms, a pinch of salt, and a few spoonfuls of water and cook for 3–5 minutes until tender. Set aside to cool, and reserve any juices from the pan. Once cool, dice the mushrooms and enough of the reserved carrots to make equal amounts. Mix together to combine.

Wearing rubber gloves, slit open the peppers in a T-shape along the length of one side. Using a teaspoon, carefully remove and discard the seeds, then fill each with the mushroom and carrot mixture until quite full. Depending on the size of the peppers, there might be some filling left over.

In a saucepan, melt the remaining 4 tablespoons (2 oz/60 g) of butter over medium–low heat. Stir in the flour, reduce the heat to low, and cook, stirring, for 1–2 minutes until it looks and smells slightly toasted. Pour in 1 cup (250 ml) of the reserved chicken stock and the reserved juices from the mushrooms and cook for 3–5 minutes to thicken. There will be some stock left over and you can add a splash more if desired. Fold in the chicken pieces and the reserved sweet potatoes and cook, stirring, to bring everything up to temperature. Transfer to a serving dish.

Serve with the stuffed peppers on the side.

Eggs Scrambled with Onions and Ground Beef

This is a rich, satisfying scrambled egg dish, brimming with distinctive savory flavors. While popular for breakfast, it is also perfect for any time of day.

SERVES 2–3

2 tablespoons sunflower, canola, or other mild vegetable oil, plus more if needed

2 oz (60 g) lean ground beef

⅓ cup (1¾ oz/50 g) finely chopped red or yellow onion

1 teaspoon finely chopped garlic

½ teaspoon *berbere* spice blend (page 40)

6 large eggs

salt and freshly ground black pepper

½ teaspoon *niter kebbeh* (page 52) or clarified butter, or more to taste

1 tablespoon finely chopped jalapeño pepper

In a sauté pan over medium heat, add 1 tablespoon of the oil and brown the ground beef. Transfer to a bowl.

In the same pan, adding more oil if necessary, cook the onion for about 5 minutes until soft and translucent. Add the garlic and cook for about 1 minute until aromatic. Season with *berbere*, add a couple of spoonfuls of water, cover, and cook over low heat for 5 minutes. Return the meat to the pan, mix well, and set aside.

In a bowl, whisk the eggs with salt and black pepper.

In a large frying pan, heat the remaining 1 tablespoon of oil over medium heat and pour in the eggs. Let them set for about 30 seconds, then add the onion and meat mixture and lightly scramble. Just before the eggs are done, stir in the *niter kebbeh* and jalapeño. Serve immediately.

Spicy Fish and Onion Stew

*As with most fish dishes in Ethiopia, Orthodox Christians largely prepare **asa wat** on fasting days (see page 93), even if extremists avoid fish as well as meat. However, outside of a fast, it is often made with an additional dollop of **niter kebbeh**, which brings a subtle lushness to the stew. While the dish is midly spicy, the flavor of the fish should still come through.*

SERVES 4

¼ cup (60 ml) sunflower, canola, or other
    mild vegetable oil

3 medium yellow onions, finely chopped
    (about 14 oz/400 g)

1 tablespoon finely chopped garlic

⅓ tablespoon grated or finely chopped ginger

½ teaspoon ground nigella seeds

¼ teaspoon ground cardamom

¼ teaspoon ground ajowan

1 tablespoon *berbere* spice blend (page 40),
    or more to taste

1 tablespoon *niter kebbeh* (page 52) or
    clarified butter, or more to taste (optional)

1½ cups (360 ml) fish stock

1 lb 5 oz (600 g) fillets of Nile perch, tilapia, or
    other firm white-fleshed fish such as halibut,
    cut into ½ x 1 inch (1 x 2.5 cm) pieces

salt and freshly ground black pepper

injera (page 20) or bread, to serve

In a large sauté pan over medium–low heat, add the oil and cook the onions for about 10 minutes until soft and translucent. Stir in the garlic and ginger and cook for about 1 minute until aromatic. Stir in the nigella, cardamom, ajowan, and *berbere*, cover, and cook over low heat for 10 minutes, stirring from time to time. Add a touch of water if needed to keep the mixture from scorching. Stir in the *niter kebbeh*, if desired. Pour in 1 cup (240 ml) of the fish stock and cook over low heat for about 8 minutes, stirring frequently, until the stock has largely reduced.

Meanwhile, in a small saucepan, bring the remaining ½ cup (120 ml) of fish stock to a boil. Cover and set aside.

Lay the fish on the onion mixture, season with salt and pepper, and cook for about 2 minutes, depending on the thickness of the fillets, until half done. Add the hot stock and cook uncovered for a further 2–3 minutes until the fish is just done. The sauce should be loose but not too runny. Serve with *injera* or a bread of your choice.

Blue Cloud Nile Perch

*While tilapia might be the species that our fishermen most frequently haul in their nets, Nile perch is usually preferred by cooks since it is better quality in both texture and taste. This contemporary fish dish combines it with one of Ethiopia's favorite breakfast dishes, **kinche** (bulgur, see page 67).*

SERVES 4–6

4¼ cups (1 liter) fish stock

2 tablespoons olive oil

½ medium yellow onion, finely chopped

2 cups (9½ oz/270 g) medium bulgur

½ tablespoon ground nigella seeds

salt

1½ cups (350 ml) heavy cream

freshly ground black pepper

1 tablespoon butter

2 sprigs of lemon thyme

1 lb 5 oz (600 g) fillets of Nile perch, tilapia, or other firm white-fleshed fish, such as halibut, cut into 4–6 pieces

½ lemon

lemon slices, to garnish (optional)

Place the stock into a saucepan and bring to a simmer. Cover and keep warm.

In a large sauté pan or wide pot over medium heat, add the oil and cook the onion for about 5 minutes until soft. Add the bulgur and cook for about 2 minutes, stirring continuously, until semi-translucent and aromatic. Stir in the nigella and cook for 1 minute, then pour in 3¾ cups (880 ml) of the stock, season with salt, and stir well. Cover and simmer for 12–15 minutes until the bulgur is tender. Add in a little more stock (or water) if needed.

Stir in ½ cup (125 ml) of the cream, season with salt and black pepper, and cook over low heat for about 2 minutes. Remove about 90 percent of the bulgur and reserve in a bowl.

Add the remaining scant 1 cup (225 ml) of cream to the pan along with ¼ cup (60 ml) of the stock and bring to a simmer over medium heat. Remove from the heat and, using an immersion hand blender, blend until frothy. Alternatively, pour into a blender and blend until frothy. Set aside.

In a large sauté pan over medium heat, add the remaining ¼ cup (60 ml) of fish stock, the butter, and a sprig of thyme, and season with salt and black pepper. When the mixture starts to simmer, add about half of the fish and cook uncovered, basting as it cooks, for about 5 minutes, depending on the size of the fillets. Turn the fish once, halfway through cooking. With a slotted spoon, transfer to a platter and cook the remaining fish. Add in a touch more stock (or water) if needed.

To serve, divide the bulgur among wide, shallow bowls and cover with the frothy sauce (reblending if needed). Place the fish on top, add a squeeze of lemon juice, and garnish with a slice of lemon, if desired.

Fish Goulash

Calling this popular fish dish a "goulash" might be a bit surprising, since it has little to do with the famous Hungarian stew, apart from perhaps its color, texture, and the inclusion of red chili peppers. However, that is the local name used for it across the country. In some places, it is not uncommon to find the dish made using strips of dried rather than fresh tilapia. You can also substitute puréed tomatoes for fresh tomatoes here, which will result in a smoother sauce.

SERVES 2–3

¼ cup (60 ml) sunflower, canola, or other mild vegetable oil, plus extra for frying

1 medium red or yellow onion, finely chopped

1 tablespoon finely chopped garlic

½ tablespoon grated or finely chopped ginger

1 teaspoon *berbere* spice blend (page 40), or more to taste

1 teaspoon ground rosemary

4 medium tomatoes, peeled, seeded, and finely chopped

salt and freshly ground black pepper

all-purpose flour, for dredging

1 lb 5 oz (600 g) fillets of Nile perch, tilapia, or other firm white-fleshed fish such as halibut, cut into 1 inch (2.5 cm) cubes

injera (page 20) or bread, to serve

In a sauté pan over medium–low heat, add the oil and cook the onion for 8–10 minutes until soft and translucent. Stir in the garlic and ginger and cook for about 1 minute until aromatic. Add the *berbere*, rosemary, and tomatoes, season with salt and black pepper, and cook over medium heat for about 10 minutes until the tomatoes have softened and lost their acidity. Add more water if needed to keep the mixture from scorching. Remove from the heat and set aside.

In a bowl, blend the flour with a few generous pinches of salt. Dredge the fish in the flour and shake off any excess.

In a large frying pan or sauté pan, heat at least ½ inch (1.5 cm) of oil until the surface shimmers, then reduce the heat to medium. Working in batches so that you do not reduce the temperature of the oil, gently lower the pieces of fish into the oil using tongs and fry for 1–2 minutes, turning once, until golden but not fully cooked. Remove with a slotted spoon and place on paper towels to drain.

Once all of the fish has been fried, transfer it to the pan and gently turn to coat in the onion and tomato sauce. Cook over medium heat until done. Serve with *injera* or a bread of your choice.

Doctor Marsamo's Fish Soup

*The popular fish market on Lake Hawassa's eastern shore has a number of stalls that
prepare freshly caught fish for customers. One is run by Marsamo Mengistu, better
known as Doctor Marsamo ("the soup doctor") who always keeps a large cauldron of fish
soup boiling away. He laces it with turmeric, ginger, garlic, and jalapeño and boils up
plenty of bones and heads of tilapia that have just been filleted out. However, the real draw
is the soup's rumored medicinal properties, which attracts a faithful crowd, ever eager
to combat a cold.*

SERVES 4

2¼ lb (1 kg) fish bones, heads, or small fish of
  white-fleshed, non-oily variety
2 tablespoons finely chopped garlic
2 tablespoons grated or finely chopped ginger
2 tablespoons finely chopped jalapeños or
  other hot fresh green chili
1 tablespoon ground turmeric
2 medium whole fish, such as sea bream, tilapia,
  or red snapper (about 1 lb/450 g each)
  cleaned; or 4 fish steaks or generous-size
  fillets
salt and freshly ground black pepper
cornbread, to serve

In a large soup pot, place the fish bones, cover with 8½ cups (2 liters) of water and
bring to a boil. Skim off any foam.

Meanwhile, in a blender or food processor, blend the garlic, ginger, and jalapeños
with a touch of the simmering fish stock, to make a thick paste. Alternatively, mash
together in a mortar with a pestle. Blend in the turmeric and spoon it all into the
pot. Partly cover the pot with a lid and simmer for 15–20 minutes.

Make a diagonal slit in the side of each fish and season with salt and black pepper.
Carefully lower the fish into the liquid and simmer for 4–8 minutes, depending on
the size of the fish, until done. When cooked, use a slotted spoon to transfer the
whole fish to a large plate and fillet, discarding the spines and heads.

To serve, place a piece of fillet in each soup bowl and ladle in plenty of broth. Serve
with cornbread.

Southern Braised Fish in a Light Garlic Ginger Sauce

My favorite traditional fish recipe, this quick dish is full of snappy flavors and textures.
***Asa** means "fish" and **lebleb** means "lightly cooked," and refers to the vegetables, which should be crunchy when eaten. The fish, too, braised in the stock, is cooked only until just done. The recipe is popular in Arba Minch ("Forty Springs"), a southwestern town about 300 miles from Addis Ababa, which sits in the foothills overlooking a spur that divides two Rift Valley lakes, Abaya and Chamo. While largely a fasting dish (see page 93), adding a dollop of **niter kebbeh** with the fish stock will give the fish extra spice flavors and a lovely glossiness.*

SERVES 4

¾ cup (175 ml) fish stock

1½ lb (700 g) fillets of Nile perch, tilapia, or other firm white-fleshed fish such as halibut, cut into 1 inch (2.5 cm) cubes

1 garlic clove, finely chopped

½ teaspoon grated or finely chopped ginger

1 medium onion, thinly sliced and separated

1 jalapeño pepper, sliced

salt

1 lemon wedge (optional)

In a large sauté pan or wide saucepan, bring the fish stock to a boil. Add the fish, cover the pan, and cook over low heat for 1 minute without stirring. Add the garlic and ginger, gently turn over the fish, and cook for a further 1 minute. Add the onion and jalapeño and gently stir without breaking up the fish. Cook until the fish is just done—about 1 minute—then season with salt and squeeze over some lemon juice, if you like, before serving straight away.

Grilled Nile Perch on a Bed of Creamy Nettles

Samma—nettles—make an ideal bed for grilled fish. However, until they have been boiled and their stingers deactivated, handle carefully and wear gloves. Nettles are in season and usually available in spring, but if they are hard to find, substitute fresh spinach leaves. Boil the spinach for just a few minutes until tender, or wilt in a covered pan over a medium–low heat.

SERVES 4–6

salt

1 lb (450 g) cleaned and trimmed tender nettle leaves

3 tablespoons olive oil

1 medium red or yellow onion, finely chopped

½ cup (125 ml) white wine

¾ cup (175 ml) heavy cream

freshly ground black pepper

1 lb 5 oz (600 g) fillets of Nile perch, tilapia, or other firm white-fleshed fish, such as halibut, cut into 4–6 pieces

juice of 1 fresh lemon

a sprig of fresh thyme

baked potatoes, or chestnut or cauliflower purée (optional), to serve

Bring a large pot of water to a boil and add a pinch of salt. Wearing gloves, add the nettles and boil for 20 minutes, then drain in a colander. The stingers deactivate through cooking and the nettles can now be handled freely. Using a wooden spoon, press firmly to remove excess liquid from the leaves and set aside.

Place a large sauté pan or wide pot over medium heat, add 1 tablespoon of the oil, and cook the onion for about 5 minutes until soft. Pour in the white wine and simmer, stirring, until the wine has reduced by half, then reduce the heat to low. Pour in the cream and allow to thicken for 1–2 minutes without letting it boil. Remove the pan from the heat, add the reserved nettles, season with salt and black pepper, and stir well. Set aside and allow the nettles to soak in the sauce.

In a large frying pan, heat the remaining 2 tablespoons of oil over high heat. Lay the perch fillets in the pan and sear on each side, turning just once. Sprinkle with the lemon juice and lay the thyme in the pan. Reduce the heat to low and cook for about 5 minutes until the fish is just done.

To serve, divide most of the nettle sauce between plates and top each with a piece of fish. Finish with a drizzle of sauce. Serve sides such as baked potatoes and puréed chestnuts or cauliflower.

8

Snacks
& Drinks

Kategna

Among the many **injera**-based snacks, **kategna** is one of the simplest—and certainly the most popular. **Injera** is usually rested for half an hour before being eaten but this recipe rubs it with **niter kebbeh** and **berbere** while still hot on the griddle and keeps cooking it until these additions have soaked through and the **injera** starts to turn crispy.

injera (page 20)
niter kebbeh (page 52) or clarified butter
berbere spice blend (page 40)

Place the *injera* on a large griddle over medium heat. Generously and evenly spread *niter kebbeh* and *berbere* over the top and cook until the butter has soaked through and the bottom is a touch crispy. Fold in half and remove from the griddle. Serve immediately.

ጬባ ወራ | CHUBA MERA

Spicy Injera Snack

This is another snack similar to **kategna** (above) but uses rested injera and a different spice blend. It comes from the area around Jimma, west of Addis Ababa, where it is served during the coffee ceremony (or with just a cup of **buna**). Some people like to spread as much as a whole cup of **niter kebbeh** over a large **injera** and, while this recipe calls for a little less, feel free to use as much as desired. Serve with coffee. Or take it "to go." Like **chicko** (see page 205), this is a **senk** dish perfect for journeys.

SERVES 4–6

3 tablespoons finely chopped jalapeño or other
   fresh hot green chili
1 heaped teaspoon finely chopped garlic
1 heaped teaspoon chopped red or yellow onion
1 heaped teaspoon grated ginger
1 heaped pressed teaspoon chopped cilantro
½ teaspoon ground ajowan
⅓ teaspoon ground nigella seeds
½ teaspoon salt
generous ¾ cup (7 oz/200 g) niter kebbeh
   (page 52) or clarified butter, at room
   temperature, or more to taste
2–3 medium injera (page 20)

In a mortar, mash the jalapeño, garlic, onion, ginger, and cilantro into a paste, and then blend in the ajowan, nigella, and salt. You should have about 5 tablespoons of paste.

Place the *niter kebbeh* in a mixing bowl, add the paste, and work it into the clarified butter.

Place one of the *injera* on a griddle and warm gently. Spread one-third of the spiced butter evenly across the top and, once melted, roll the flatbread and cut into pieces about 4 inches (10 cm) wide.

Grill the remaining *injera* with the rest of the spread and serve.

Helemur

Helemur is a Berta tribe tradition in Benishangul-Gumz. This recipe is very similar to alabere—a traditional cornflakes-type meal—but differs in that the soaked dough is removed from the final result, which is consumed purely as a drink. The dough is layered thickly on the pan to allow the bottom part to roast, which brings a tea-like color to the beverage. Packed with minerals and sugar, and prepared in liquid form, this is an ideal appetizer for individuals who haven't eaten all day. Helemur is a perfect transition to more solid food selections in periods of prolonged fasting like Ramadan.

SERVES 4–6

2 cups (8½ oz/240 g) pearl millet flour

¾ cup (4½ oz/125 g) malted barley flour

1 teaspoon ground nigella seeds

1 teaspoon ground cinnamon

1 teaspoon ground cloves

1 teaspoon ground fenugreek

sunflower, canola, or other mild vegetable oil for oiling

3 tablespoons white sugar

In a mixing bowl, blend the flours. Add the nigella, cinnamon, cloves, and fenugreek, and begin working in 2 cups (500 ml) of water. Blend until it is a smooth paste without lumps. Cover with a dishcloth and let it rest overnight in a warm place, 85–90°F (30–32°C).

Moisten a paper towel with oil and wipe the surface of a non-stick crêpe pan or skillet, or large, traditional *mitad*. Place over medium heat.

Working in batches, thinly spread the dough on the pan. Leave to cook and stick a bit, 2–3 minutes, before peeling or scraping it off and placing in a bowl. Turn as needed so that it is completely cooked. It might break apart, which is fine. Place in a bowl. Once cool, crumble or shred the pieces.

Dissolve the sugar in 2 cups (500 ml) warm water, or heat as necessary in a saucepan.

Pour the syrup over the cooked dough in the bowl, turn to submerge, and set aside to soak for 30 minutes. Strain, reserving the liquid. Squeeze out as much liquid as possible. Discard the solids. Serve the reserved liquid in glasses.

Kolo

*Kolo is by far the most famous, easiest to prepare, and easiest to offer Ethiopian snack. Traditionally, it is toasted on a wide iron pan, stirring with a curved iron stick to avoid burning. Considering the **kolo** market is locally very popular and has grown and become an export item, it is nowadays prepared using sand and sieves. The sand is first brought to an overwhelming high temperature over an iron **mitad** (see page 10). Then barley seeds are added in bulk before they are rapidly mixed, using two curved iron sticks, for no more than 10 seconds. With the same speed, the mixture is transferred to a wide sieve that is shaken to strain the fine sand and salvage the roasted grains. The roasted barley is then mixed with safflower seeds, peanuts, and sometimes desi chickpeas. Note that safflower seeds are commonly used in our traditional recipes; they can easily be substituted with sunflower seeds.*

SERVES 6–8

scant 2 cups (13 oz/375 g) pearl barley

scant 1 cup (4½ oz/125 g) shelled peanuts

½ tablespoon shelled sunflower seeds

salt

Roast the barley. Place the grains in a large, dry frying pan over medium heat. Toast, stirring frequently, until the barley turns a rich brown and has a lovely nutty aroma, 10–15 minutes. Be careful not to scorch. Transfer to a bowl.

Alternatively, preheat the oven to 300°F (150°C). Place the barley on a baking try and bake, stirring the barley from time to time, until it turns a rich brown and has a lovely nutty aroma, about 20 minutes. Be careful not to scorch. Transfer to a mixing bowl.

In the frying pan, add the peanuts, and toast over medium heat until warm, about 5 minutes. Transfer to the bowl. Add the sunflower seeds to the frying pan and toast until warm, about 3 minutes. Add to the bowl.

Season with salt and toss to blend. Let cool before serving.

Rich Barley Flour Squares

This popular snack is deliciously rich and decadent. However, while the texture is a bit like halva, and people often refer to it as "local chocolate," don't expect it to be sweet. This is a cuisine virtually free of sugar. It should stick to the roof of the mouth when you eat it—that is part of its pleasure.

*Chicko is made with **beso** flour—barley that has been roasted before being milled. Since it is nearly impossible to find outside Ethiopia, the best alternative is to toast pearl barley and then grind it in an electric spice or coffee grinder. Some cooks like to add spices— cardamom, cloves, black pepper—to the **niter kebbeh** before working it into the flour, and just like oil in mayonnaise, limitless amounts of **niter kibbeh** can be added into **chicko**, so adjust to your taste.*

*Serve with strong black coffee or wrap it up to take on a road trip, since it is what is known as a **senk** item. **Senk** is an Amharic word that refers to food that is made to eat on long journeys.*

MAKES ABOUT 24 SQUARES

1 cup (7 oz/200 g) pearl barley

scant ½ cup (3½ oz/100 g) *niter kebbeh* (page 52) or clarified butter, at room temperature

spices of your choice (optional)

2 generous pinches of salt

Place the barley in a large, dry frying pan over medium heat. Toast, stirring frequently, for 10–15 minutes until the grains turn a rich brown and release a lovely nutty aroma. Be careful not to scorch. Transfer to a plate and let cool. Alternatively, preheat the oven to 300°F (150°C) and roast the barley on a baking tray for about 20 minutes, stirring or shaking it from time to time.

Working in batches, grind the roasted barley into flour in an electric spice or coffee grinder. Pass it through a sieve to remove any grainy bits and regrind. You should have about 1½ cups (6½ oz/185 g) of fine flour.

Place the *niter kebbeh* in a bowl, along with the spices of your choice. Sift in about half of the flour and the salt, and work with your hands until you have a moist, thick dough that doesn't crumble. Add the remaining flour as required—there might be some left over.

Place the dough on a plate, press out until it is about ½ inch (1.5 cm) thick, and cut into 1 inch (2.5 cm) squares. Either serve straight away or cover with plastic wrap and store in the refrigerator. Always allow time for the squares to come back to room temperature before serving.

Buna

There are just two species of coffee widely cultivated today, Arabica (*Coffea Arabica*) and the heartier Robusta (*Coffea Canephora*). Arabica is the most prevalent and superior of the two, with finer, more nuanced flavors and higher prices on the international market. But, *Coffea Arabica* is not actually from Arabia, as its name suggests—bestowed on it by the Swedish taxonomist Carlus Linnaeus in 1753. Instesd, Arabica's center of origin is the montane forests of Ethiopia. Predominately in the cool, cloud forests of Kafa and Jimma in the southwest of the country. Multiple varieties exist within the Arabica coffee species, and 5,046 have been documented in Ethiopia.

Nowhere is coffee's importance more evident than in Ethiopia. The coffee sector contributes up to 10 percent of Ethiopia's GDP, and provides livelihoods for approximately fifteen million Ethiopian smallhold farmers across the country.

But coffee goes much deeper than economics here. Ethiopia is the largest producer of coffee in Africa, and the third largest producer of Arabica in the world. Yet it exports under 50 percent of the amount it grows. To put that into perspective, Kenya consumes just 3 percent of its own production and Colombia exports 86 percent of its beans.

Coffee is not just Ethiopia's national drink, but it is a staple of the country. It is drunk throughout the day—but never alone. Every meeting includes coffee, and coffee always requires company. *Buna tetu*, which means "come drink coffee," is a famous communal tradition in Ethiopia, where children are sent to knock on neighbors' doors to fetch occupants and invite them to share coffee. This bonding culture is a key component that shapes our social lifestyle.

Preparing a traditional cup of *buna* can take an hour, and drinking it can take several more—sometimes a total of 4 to 5 hours, especially during festivities. The process begins with washing and roasting the beans on iron *mitad* (see page 10). When evenly roasted, the young lady preparing coffee in *habesha kemis* (traditional clothes) hurries to take the *mitad* to her guests, while an enchanting smoke is still being released

from the beans. Guests stop their conversation and, one by one, with one hand movement, blow the smoke towards their nose and take a few deep breaths to welcome freshly roasted coffee. This is the second phase of Ethiopian coffee sensory experience.

The beans are then brewed in a traditional mortar before putting them in a *jebena*, in which water has already been set to boil. *Jebena*, a traditional clay pot made specifically for preparing coffee, comes in various different shapes and sizes. From the one-hole *jebena* typically used in north and west Ethiopia, to the two narrow-hole *jebena* of the central highlands, to the wide two-hole *jebena* of the south (especially around Hossana), and even to the less common and mystical three hole *jebena*, the clay pots hold essential value in every Ethiopian household.

Having added brewed coffee to the simmering water, and once coffee foam discharges from the top hole of the *jebena*, it is removed from heat and left to allow all the solid coffee particles to settle at the bottom.

The last phase of the Ethiopian coffee sensory experience begins when the clinking sound of *sini* (coffee cups) is heard. Once all the cups are gathered on the *rekebot*–the coffee platter coffee is poured into the first cup, which culturally is not for consumption but to confirm the murky liquid is free of coffee dabs. The drinking ceremony can finally begin, and coffee is offered with multiple seasoning options, including sugar, salt, *rue*, or *niter kebbeh* (see page 208).

Chicko (see page 205), *Defo dabo* (see page 28), and popcorn, in cups, are displayed as coffee snacks on *ketema*, freshly cut grass, displayed both on the floor and tables (see image on page 208). Conversations start to warm up while lingering sweet incense dissipates in the room. From *abol* (first coffee cup) to *tona* (second cup), and finally *bereka* (last cup), the *jebena* is refilled until the settled coffee bits squeeze out their every last taste and guests are finally satisfied. This is my favorite tradition.

Cascara Coffee Husk Infusion

*After the coffee fruit (or cherry) is picked, the outer husk gets peeled away to reveal a pair of seeds—the beans—and often, that fruit peel is discarded. However, for centuries, people in Harar have known that these leathery peels contain sweet, fruity notes of hibiscus, cherry, rosehip, and even curing tobacco, and have used them to prepare **ashara** infusions, enhanced even further by the addition of cardamom or cinnamon. Recently, cascara or "coffee cherry tea" has begun appearing on North American and European café menus, and coffee companies are beginning to sell the dried husks to prepare the infusion at home. Steep like a tisane and sweeten with honey.*

SERVES 1

1 tablespoon cascara or dried coffee husks (about 5 g)

2–3 green cardamom pods

honey

Rinse out a stovetop teapot or saucepan with hot water and drop in the cascara. Crush the cardamom pods between thumb and forefinger and add to the pot.

Pour 1 cup (250 ml) of boiling water into the teapot, cover, and steep for 3–5 minutes. Strain the infusion into a glass and sweeten with honey.

Green Coffee Beans Cooked in Butter

Pan-roasted coffee beans make a simple, common snack in Ethiopia and are a delight to crunch on, like nuts. In Jimma, the largest city in the southwest of the country, they are also part of every wedding celebration. The bride's family prepares them for the groom's family and then, when the first child is born, that role is reversed and the groom's family prepares the beans for their in-laws.

Buna kela takes time to cook slowly until the beans become brittle and crunchy—rather than hard and inedible. It is imperative to use the lowest heat possible and to let the beans absorb the butter before adding more. Both fresh coffee beans and dried coffee beans are used to make buna kela in Jimma, but fresh ones are preferred when they are available during the coffee-harvesting season. The flavor of this snack is sharp and bitter—a treat for lovers of dark roasted coffee.

MAKES ABOUT 1¾ oz (50 g)

1¾ oz (50 g) green coffee beans

3 tablespoons *niter kebbeh* (page 52) or clarified butter, plus extra if needed

a pinch of ground nigella seeds

3 cardamom pods, seeds removed and pods discarded

1–2 lemongrass stems, split lengthways into 6–9 pieces

a pinch of grated or finely chopped fresh ginger

salt

Place the coffee in a large bowl of water and pick over, discarding any debris or defective beans. Drain and spread out on paper towels to dry.

In a small, heavy-bottomed saucepan, add the beans with 1 tablespoon of the *niter kebbeh* and cook over the lowest possible heat, stirring frequently. Once the beans have absorbed the butter, add another 1 tablespoon of *niter kebbeh* and cook over the lowest heat for 1 hour, stirring from time to time.

Stir in the remaining 1 tablespoon of *niter kebbeh* and the nigella, cardamom seeds, and about one-third of the lemongrass. Cook, partly covered, for 30 minutes, then remove the lemongrass and discard. Add another one-third of the lemongrass and cook for about 15 minutes until the beans are brittle and crunchy—they should be a rich, dark brown and make a hollow sound when stirred. Remove and discard the lemongrass.

Stir in the ginger, a pinch of salt, and more *niter kebbeh* if needed. Add the remaining lemongrass and cook for a final 5 minutes. Spoon into a small serving bowl and allow to cool for a few minutes. Serve hot or cold with small spoons.

Abesh Wuha

*Abesh Wuha is an esteemed festive tradition from Argoba. Argoba is part of the glorious Yefat dynasty, an ancient kingdom of Ethiopia following the Axumit dynasty. It is a holy land where the tombs of the first messengers of Prophet Mohammed can be found. There, where most habitants are Muslim, **Abesh Wuha** is a favorite non-alcoholic beverage and it is prepared during weddings and special occasions. Traditionally, preparing **Abesh Wuha** ("Fenugreek Water" as it translates literally) takes between 10–15 days, and multiple techniques are used to create a harmony of various tastes and aromas. Here, a simple version of the recipe allows you to prepare a version of the beverage in only one evening. See the recipe for Smoked Milk or Water, page 160, for details and instructions on smoking with olive wood.*

MAKES ABOUT 2 LITERS

1 cup (4½ oz/125 g) pearl millet flour

1 tablespoon ground fenugreek
  or more to taste

2–4 small olive wood twigs
  or smoking chips

1 tablespoon ground nigella seeds

1 tablespoon runny honey

1 teaspoon ground ginger

1 teaspoon ground cinnamon

½ teaspoon ground green cardamom

½ teaspoon ground cloves

Heat an ungreased skillet over medium-low heat, add the flour, and lightly dry-toast until aromatic, about 5–10 minutes, stirring and shaking the pan. Transfer to a bowl. Add the fenugreek to the skillet and toast until warm and aromatic, about 1 minute, and transfer to the bowl. Mix together.

In a large saucepan, bring 4¼ cups (1 liter) of water to a boil over high heat. Stir in the flour and fenugreek blend, reduce the heat to low, and cook 30 minutes, stirring frequently to keep from scorching. Stir in a touch more water if needed.

Meanwhile, smoke a large plastic pot that will hold at least 4 quarts (4 liters) using an olive tree twig following the directions on page 160. Add 12¾ cups (3 liters) water to the smoked pot.

Stir in the boiling flour mixture and add the nigella. Cover and keep in a cool place overnight.

The next day, without disturbing the settled solids, pour off the liquid into a clean pitcher or jug. Stir in the honey, ginger, cinnamon, cardamom, and cloves.

Before serving, smoke the empty serving glasses with olive wood and then pour in some of the drink.

Layered Fruit Juice

*Spris have become extremely popular in Ethiopia and in Ethiopian restaurants abroad, since the colors of the puréed fruit recall the country's green, yellow, and red flag. While considered a juice, the texture is so thick that it needs to be eaten with a spoon. Those who are patient work slowly through each layer, while others immediately blend them together. Add a spoonful of sugar or honey if you want to sweeten it up, although the best **spris** houses in Soderc near Awash hardly use sweeteners other than Vimto, a British soft drink, which creates a stunning color contrast. If you can find it, you can add 2 teaspoons of Vimto between each layer of fruit. Chill the fruit before peeling for a fresher juice.*

SERVES 4

2 ripe medium avocados

½ ripe medium papaya

3 ripe medium mangoes

1 lime, cut in half

Peel and pit the avocados. In a food processer, blend with ½ cup (125 ml) of water to a smooth purée. Divide between four glasses.

Peel and seed the papaya and cut into large pieces. Clean the food processor and blend the papaya to a smooth purée. Divide between the glasses to create a second layer.

Peel and cut away the flesh on the mangoes. Clean the food processor and blend the mango to a smooth purée. Divide between the glasses for the third layer.

Squeeze a lime over the top of each glass and serve immediately with long-handled spoons.

Date and Orange Marmalade

During the month of Ramadan, when Muslims fast from sunrise to sunset, many market stalls around the country are piled high with dates, since they are the first item eaten with the breaking of the fast. It is tradition (Mohammed broke the fast with a date) but they also help prepare the empty stomach for the (large) meal ahead. While most dates sold are North African imports, Ethiopia has its own palm groves in the Asayta, the Oasis of Afar. The local variety tends to be thinner and crunchier than the classic soft, wrinkly dates. This marmalade—sweet and rich, with a lovely background of orange bitterness—is a way to preserve the pleasure of the dates a bit longer. Spread on toast, dollop in yogurt, or eat with a bowl of oatmeal.

MAKES ABOUT 1 LB 10 oz (750 g)

1 lb 2 oz (500 g) fresh dates, unpitted
3–4 ripe medium oranges
½ ripe lemon
2 tablespoons clear honey

Wipe the dates with a damp cloth and remove the pits. Wipe the oranges and, working over a bowl to catch all the juices, cut into thin slices, removing all the seeds. Zest the lemon and reserve.

In a large, heavy-bottomed saucepan, add the dates, oranges, and any juice. Cover with 1½ cups (350 ml) of water and bring to a boil. Add the honey and lemon zest and squeeze in the lemon juice. Cover the pot, reduce the heat to low, and cook for 2 hours, stirring frequently, until it forms a paste. Add more water as needed to keep the marmalade from scorching.

Remove the pan from the heat and set aside to cool. Purée using a handheld immersion blender or food processor. The mixture should be smooth and thick, but not unwieldy. Add a touch of water if necessary.

Spoon into clean preserving jars, leaving about ½ inch (1.5 cm) of space at the top. Wipe the jars clean, cover, and store in the refrigerator. Consume within 2–3 weeks.

Habesha Spicy Puff Pastry with Fresh Whipped Cream and Mulberries

Injore is the local name for white mulberries, a fruit easily found everywhere in town during my childhood. Now more scarce, this local variety of mulberry, with a touch of tartness, combines well with puff pastry, a light dusting of spicy **mitmita** (see page 47) and creamy, cool fresh whipped cream. Use blackberries, raspberries, small strawberries, or ripe mulberries if you can't find white mulberries.

Preheat the oven to 350°F (180°C) and line a baking sheet with parchment paper.

Roll out the pastry if needed to a 12 inch (30 cm) square piece, place on the prepared baking sheet, and use a fine-mesh sieve to lightly dust with *mitmita*. Place a square of parchment paper on top, then cover the paper with a layer of baking weights (or dried beans or rice) to keep the pastry flat during cooking.

Bake for about 20 minutes until golden on the bottom. Remove the weights and cook for a further 5–10 minutes until crispy, flipping it over if necessary.

While still warm, cut the pastry into 2 x 4 inch (5 x 10 cm) rectangles—you should have 18 pieces. Place the whipped cream into a pastry bag with a medium tip.

Assemble the pastries. On top of a rectangle of pastry, arrange three berries down each side, squeeze some whipped cream in the middle, sprinkle with a pinch of cinnamon, and top with another piece of pastry. Repeat to make a second layer, then dust with confectioner's sugar. Repeat until all the pastries have been assembled, and serve.

SERVES 6

7 oz (200 g) ready-made puff pastry dough (about ½ package)
mitmita spice blend (page 47)
fresh whipped cream
1 lb (450 g) fresh white mulberries (*injore*), blackberries, raspberries, or small whole hulled strawberries
ground cinnamon
confectioner's sugar

Lacy Ethiopian Tuiles with Toasted Barley

*Ethiopia is a largely sugar-free cuisine and even **buna kurs**—Ethiopian coffee snacks—
are savory. Among the most popular are toasted barley grains, also known as **kolo**.
These classic French **tuiles** ("tiles") incorporate barley into their sugary lace for a sweet
buna kurs.*

In a dry frying pan over medium heat, add the barley, cover, and cook for
4–5 minutes until toasted and pleasantly crunchy. Keep the pan covered as
the barley will "pop" around, but watch that it doesn't scorch. Set aside.

In a mixing bowl, blend the confectioner's sugar, flour, peanuts, and lemon zest. Stir
in the orange and lime or lemon juices and then the roasted barley. Pour in the
butter and stir to blend the mixture.

Transfer the mixture to a pastry bag or cover the bowl with plastic wrap and
refrigerate until thoroughly chilled.

Preheat the oven to 350°F (180°C) and line two baking trays with parchment paper
or silicone baking mats.

Using a teaspoon or a pastry bag, place small dollops of the mixture at least 6 inches
(16 cm) apart to allow them to spread (they will flatten to about 3 inch/8 cm each in
the oven). Bake for 10 minutes until deep, golden brown—watch carefully at the end
to avoid burning.

While the cookies are still flexible, drape them over a rolling pin (or glass bottle)
covered with foil to form a curled shape. They will stiffen within a few seconds, so
work quickly. Once stiff, arrange on a sheet of parchment paper until ready to serve.

Repeat with the remaining batter, allowing the trays to cool between batches.

MAKES ABOUT 24 COOKIES

2½ tablespoons barley
1 cup (3½ oz/100 g) confectioner's sugar
3½ tablespoons all-purpose flour
3 tablespoons ground peanuts
zest of ½ lemon
2 teaspoons freshly squeezed orange juice
2 teaspoons freshly squeezed lime or
    lemon juice
2 tablespoons butter, melted

Index

Note: page numbers in *italics* refer to illustrations.

abesha wuha 211
abish wat 132, *133*
aioli, spicy aioli 34
ajowan (bishop's weed) 10, 28, 38, 68, 102, 152–4, 156–7, 170, 187, 198
   berbere spice blend 40, 43
   mitmita spice blend 47
Amharic language 11
asa goulash 189
asa lebleb 192, *193*
asa shorba 190, *191*
asa wat 187
ashara 209
atakilt 79
ater kik alicha 102
ater wat fitfit 68, *69*
awaze dipping sauce 45, 116, 128
   raw beef with four dipping sauces 147
   sizzling beef strips with awaze chili sauce 130
ayib 78, 86
azifa 104, *105*

banana and flaxseed purée 72, *73*
banana leaf, whole-grain bread baked in banana leaves 28, *29*
   barley, lacy Ethiopian tuiles with toasted barley 218, *219*
barley flour 201
barley porridge with niter kebbeh and served with yogurt 58
bean(s) 83
   breakfast fava beans *62*, 63
   kidney bean and okra stew with cornmeal patties 112, *113*
   sautéed string beans and carrots 89
béchamel sauce 120
beef 140, 141
   beef tripe and tongue 143
   buttery spiced raw tenderloin 142
   collard greens with beef stew 127
   cubed sirloin with onions and jalapeño peppers 128, *129*
   dried beef stew with onions, peppers, spices, and dried *injera* 136, *137*
   eggs scrambled with onions and ground beef 185
   fried beef with onions 131
   ground prime beef in spicy fenugreek sauce 126
   lentil soup with spicy dried beef and crispy leeks 106, *107*
   raw beef with four dipping sauces 147
   sizzling beef strips with awaze chili sauce 130
   spicy beef and fenugreek stew with potatoes 132, *133*
   spicy beef stew with barley dough *138*, 139
   steak tartar with spiced clarified butter 144, *145*
   tenderloin with coffee sauce 148
beet, braised beet batons with jalapeño peppers 76, *77*
beg enfele 156–7, *158–9*
beg siga alicha 152
bekel tibs 164, 165
berbere deleh paste 43, 44
berbere spice blend 6, 10, 33, 40, 58, 64, 71, 94, 107, 118, 126, 132, 136, 139, 151, 156–7, 174, 178, 185, 187, 189, 198
   awaze dipping sauce 45
   berbere deleh paste 43, 44
   recipe *41*, *42–3*
berz 173
besobela (Ethiopian basil) 38, 112
   berbere spice blend 40, 42
   fresh chili dipping sauce 55
   niter kebbeh 52
bread
   spicy shepherds' bread 33
   whole-grain bread baked in banana leaves 28, *29*
   see also flatbread; *injera* (flatbread)
bula 30
bula genfo 30
bulgur 188
   simple fasting bulgur 67
buna (coffee) 206–7
buna kela 210
buttermilk 139
   buttermilk-marinated chicken with grilled vegetables 178, *179*

cabbage
   cabbage rolls with lamb tongue 154, *155*
   potatoes and cabbage in ginger turmeric sauce 79
cardamom 94, 209–11
   berbere spice blend 40
   mekelesha spice blend 44
   niter kebbeh 52
carrot 83, 181, 184
   goat in mild turmeric stew with carrots 153
   potatoes and carrots in an onion turmeric sauce 88
   sautéed string beans and carrots 89

teff tagliatelle with sprouted fenugreek and carrots 122, *123*
chechebsa 64, *65*
cheese 48
   Ethiopian gnocchi 119
   homemade fresh cheese 78
   moringa teff lasagne 120
   shiro salad 98
   teff tagliatelle with sprouted fenugreek and carrots 122
   whole-grain teff salad 86
"Chef Yohanis Qegnet" (TV show) 8
chicken
   buttermilk-marinated chicken with grilled vegetables 178, *179*
   chicken simmered in a mild onion and turmeric sauce *176*, 177
   chicken in *tej* sauce with oranges 174, *175*
   creamy chicken and sweet potatoes with stuffed green chilies 184
   nigella-glazed roast chicken and black and white sesame seeds *180*, 181
   slow-cooked spicy chicken with hard-boiled eggs 170, *171*
chicko 204, 205
chickpea flour 98, *114*, 115
   spicy chickpea flour stew *114*, 115
chickpea with spicy flaxseed paste 116, *117*
chili
   berbere spice blend 40
   creamy chicken and sweet potatoes with stuffed green chilies 184
   fresh chili dipping sauce 55, 147
   Mareko chili 42
   mitmita spice blend 47
Christianity 9, 92–3, 108, 140
chuba mera 198
cinnamon 201, 211, 217
   berbere spice blend 40
   mekelesha spice blend 44
clove 38, 201, 211
   berbere spice blend 40
   mekelesha spice blend 44
coffee 6, 108, 206–7
   cascara coffee husk infusion *208*, 209
   green coffee beans cooked in butter 210
   tenderloin with coffee sauce 148
collard greens
   collard greens with beef stew 127
   collard greens with onions and fresh ginger 80, *81*
   collard greens with spiced butter and *mitmita* 82

coriander seed 38
    niter kebbeh 52
cornmeal patties with kidney bean and okra
    stew 112, *113*
cream desserts, *habesha* spicy puff pastry with
    fresh whipped cream and mulberries *216, 217*
cumin 38, 132, 154, 165, 177

daata (fresh chili dipping sauce) 55, 147
date and orange marmalade 214
dinich alicha 88
dipping sauces
    fresh chili dipping sauce 55, 147
    see also awaze dipping sauce
dirkosh quanta firfir 136, *137*
doro alicha 176, 177
doro effeta (oil from cooking *doro wat*) 166
doro wat 170, *171*
dressing, flaxseed 66
duba wat 70, *71*
dulet 149

egg
    breakfast fava beans 63
    doro alicha 177
    eggs scrambled with onions and ground beef 185
    Ethiopian gnocchi 119
    flatbread pastries stuffed with egg 60, *61*
    pasta dough 120, 122
    shiro salad 98
    slow-cooked spicy chicken with hard-boiled
        eggs 170, *171*
    spicy aioli 34
enset 30
Ethiopian history 9, 140–1
Ethiopian Orthodox Christian Church 92–3, 108

fasting 93, 108, 140
fava bean, breakfast fava beans *62*, 63
fayal kikil 153
fenugreek seed 38, 108, 139, 201, 211
    berbere deleh paste 44
    ground prime beef in spicy fenugreek sauce 126
    niter kebbeh 48
    spicy beef and fenugreek stew with potatoes
        132, *133*
    teff tagliatelle with sprouted fenugreek and
        carrots 122, *123*
fetira 59
fetira be enkulal 60, *61*
fish
    blue cloud Nile perch 188

Doctor Marsamo's fish soup 190, *191*
fish goulash 189
grilled Nile perch on a bed of creamy nettles
    194, *195*
southern braised fish in a light garlic ginger
    sauce *192*, 193
spicy fish and onion stew 187
flatbread
    butter-soaked flatbread 64, *65*
    flatbread pastries stuffed with egg 60, *61*
    layered flatbread pastries with honey 59
    round flatbread 32
    see also injera (flatbread)
flaxseed
    chickpeas with spicy flaxseed paste 116, *117*
    flaxseed and banana purée 72, *73*
    torn *injera* with flaxseed dressing 66
foselia sautéed string beans and carrots 89
fruit juice, layered *212, 213*
ful 62, 63

garlic 28, 38–9
    berbere spice blend 40, 42
    Southern braised fish in a light garlic ginger
        sauce *192, 193*
    spicy aioli 34
Geez language 11, 92
genfo 58
ginger 39
    berbere spice blend 40, 42
    collard greens with onions and fresh ginger 80, *81*
    potatoes and cabbage in ginger turmeric
        sauce 79
    southern braised fish in a light garlic ginger
        sauce *192, 193*
    yellow split peas in a mild ginger and onion
        sauce 102
gnocchi, Ethiopian 119
goat
    Afar roasted leg of kid goat with yellow rice
        164, 165
    goat in mild turmeric stew with carrots 153
gomen 80, *81*
gomen be sega 127
gomen kitfo 82
gored-gored 142
goulash, fish 189
grinders, electric 11

habesha spicy puff pastry with fresh whipped
    cream and mulberries *216, 217*
Harar 9, 108

hazo 48
helemur 200, 201
honey 59, 64, 209, 211, 214
    awaze dipping sauce 45
    niter kebbeh 48
hyena feeding ritual 108

injera (flatbread) 6, 10, 16–17
    abset technique 16–17
    doro alicha 177
    dried beef stew with onions, peppers, spices,
        and dried *injera* 136, *137*
    fish goulash 189
    goat in mild turmeric stew with carrots 153
    kategna 198
    one-day *injera* 24, *25*
    raw beef with four dipping sauces 147
    shiro salad 98
    slow-cooked spicy chicken with hard-boiled
        eggs 170
    spicy beef and fenugreek stew with potatoes 132
    spicy fish and onion stew 187
    spicy *injera* snack 198
    spicy tomato stew 71
    torn *injera* with flaxseed dressing 66
    traditional *injera* 20–1, *22–3*
    whole dried peas with cut *injera* 68, *69*
Islam 9, 108

jalapeño pepper
    braised beet batons with jalapeño peppers 76,
        77
    cubed sirloin with onions and jalapeño
        peppers 128, *129*
jebena (clay coffee pot) 207
Judaism 9, 92, 141

kategna 198
khat 108
kidney bean and okra stew with cornmeal
    patties 112, *113*
kinche 67
kitfo 48, 144, *145*
kocko 30
kolo 202, *203*
korerima 39, 43, 48
koseret 10, 39
    mitmita spice blend 47
    niter kebbeh 48, 52
kulet 11
kupe 112, *113*
kurt 140, 141, 147

lamb
 cabbage rolls with lamb tongue 154
 festive dipped leg of lamb 156–7, 158–9
 lamb-stuffed vegetables 166, 167
 spicy lamb stew 150, 151
 tender lamb cubes simmered in mild turmeric
  and onion sauce 152
 three-meat minced lamb 149
lasagne, *moringa* teff lasagne 120, 121
leek, lentil soup with spicy dried beef and crispy
 leeks 106, 107
lentil
 Lenten lentil salad with mustard 104, 105
 lentil soup with spicy dried beef and crispy
  leeks 106, 107
 spicy red lentils 118
long pepper 39, 43
 mekelesha spice blend 44

marmalade, date and orange marmalade 214
mekelesha spice blend 44, 118, 126, 132, 151, 170
melas sember 143
milk 72, 98, 119, 120
 creamy scalloped potatoes with smoked milk
  162, 163
 homemade fresh cheese 78
 smoked milk or water 160, 161
millet flour (pearl) 201, 211
minchet abish 126
misr wat 118
mitad (griddle) 10–11, 17, 206–7
mitmita spice blend 10, 34, 42, 86, 119, 127, 131,
 143, 144, 145, 147, 149, 217
 collard greens with spiced butter and *mitmita* 82
 recipe 46, 47
mitten shiro 34, 98, 103
monasteries 92–3
moringa leaf 98
 moringa teff lasagne 120, 121
mulberry, *habesha* spicy puff pastry with fresh
 whipped cream and mulberries 216, 217
Muslims 108
 see also Islam
mustard 34, 83, 147
 homemade Ethiopian brown mustard 54
 Lenten lentil salad with mustard 104, 105

nettle, grilled Nile perch on a bed of creamy
 nettles 194, 195
nigella seed 10, 28, 32, 39, 118, 126, 132, 151, 170,
 187–8, 198, 201, 210–11
 berbere spice blend 40, 43

mitmita spice blend 47
nigella-glazed roast chicken and black and
 white sesame seeds 180, 181
niter kebbeh 52
Nile perch
 blue cloud Nile perch 188
 fish goulash 189
 grilled Nile perch on a bed of creamy nettles
  194, 195
 southern braised fish in a light garlic ginger
  sauce 193
 spicy fish and onion stew 187
niter kebbeh (Ethiopian spiced clarified butter)
 6, 10, 11, 48, 52, 53
 barley porridge with *niter kebbeh* and served
  with yogurt 58
 beef tripe and tongue 143
 butter-soaked flatbread 64
 buttermilk-marinated chicken with grilled
  vegetables 178
 buttery spiced raw tenderloin 142
 collard greens with beef stew 127
 collard greens with spiced butter and
  mitmita 82
 doro alicha 177
 dried beef stew with onions, peppers, spices,
  and dried *injera* 136
 eggs scrambled with onions and ground beef 185
 festive dipped leg of lamb 156–7
 fried beef with onions 131
 goat in mild turmeric stew with carrots 153
 green coffee beans cooked in butter 210
 ground prime beef in spicy fenugreek sauce 126
 kategna 198
 rich barley flour squares 205
 sizzling beef strips with *awaze* chili sauce 130
 slow-cooked spicy chicken with hard-boiled
  eggs 170
 smooth *shiro* 103
 spicy beef stew with barley dough 139
 spicy chickpea flour stew 115
 spicy fish and onion stew 187
 spicy *injera* snack 198
 spicy lamb stew 151
 steak tartar with spiced clarified butter 144, 145
 tender lamb cubes simmered in mild turmeric
  and onion sauce 152
 three-meat minced lamb 149

oat(s), thin flat oat cakes 26, 27
okra and kidney bean stew with cornmeal
 patties 112, 113

onion
 berbere spice blend 40
 chicken simmered in a mild onion and
  turmeric sauce 176, 177
 collard greens with onions and fresh ginger
  80, 81
 cubed sirloin with onions and jalapeño
  peppers 128, 129
 dried beef stew with onions, peppers, spices,
  and dried *injera* 136, 137
 eggs scrambled with onions and ground beef 185
 fried beef with onions 131
 lamb-stuffed vegetables 166
 potatoes and carrots in an onion turmeric
  sauce 88
 spicy fish and onion stew 187
 tender lamb cubes simmered in mild turmeric
  and onion sauce 152
 yellow split peas in a mild ginger and onion
  sauce 102
orange 218
 chicken in *tej* sauce with oranges 174, 175
 date and orange marmalade 214

pasta
 moringa teff lasagne 120, 121
 teff tagliatelle with sprouted fenugreek and
  carrots 122
pastries
 flatbread pastries stuffed with egg 60, 61
 habesha spicy puff pastry with fresh whipped
  cream and mulberries 216, 217
 layered flatbread pastries with honey 59
patties, kidney bean and okra stew with
 cornmeal patties 112, 113
Paul Bocuse Institute 8
peanut 112, 202, 218
pearl barley 202
 rich barley flour squares 204, 205
 spicy beef stew with barley dough 138, 139
pea(s)
 whole dried peas with cut *injera* 68, 69
 yellow split peas in a mild ginger and onion
  sauce 102
pepper 90, 98
 dried beef stew with onions, peppers, spices,
  and dried *injera* 136, 137
 lamb-stuffed vegetables 166
 stuffed hot green peppers 96, 97
 see also long pepper
porridge, barley porridge with *niter kebbeh* and
 served with yogurt 58

potato 181
    creamy scalloped potatoes with smoked milk 162, *163*
    lamb-stuffed vegetables 166
    potatoes and cabbage in ginger turmeric sauce 79
    potatoes and carrots in an onion turmeric sauce 88
    spicy beef and fenugreek stew with potatoes 132, *133*
pumpkin, spicy pumpkin stew 94, *95*

rice, Afar roasted leg of kid goat with yellow rice *164*, 165
rue (herb of grace) 39, 42, 55

salads
    Lenten lentil salad with mustard 104, *105*
    shiro salad 98, *99*
    tomato salad 90, *91*
    vegetable salad 83
    whole-grain teff salad 86, *87*
sausage, *shiro* sliders with fresh sausage 34, *35*
seasonings 37–55
senafich 54
senig 96, 97
shekla tibs 128, *129*
shimbra wat 116, *117*
shiro
    shiro flours 10, 115, 126
    shiro salad 98, *99*
    shiro sliders with fresh sausage 34, *35*
    shiro wat 114, 115
    smooth *shiro* 103
siga tibs 131
sils 70, 71
smoked milk or water 160, *161*
soup
    Doctor Marsamo's fish soup 190, *191*
    lentil soup with spicy dried beef and crispy leeks *106*, 107
spices 10
    Ethiopian spice box 38–9
    see also specific spices
stews
    collard greens with beef stew 127
    dried beef stew with onions, peppers, spices, and dried *injera* 136, *137*
    goat in mild turmeric stew with carrots 153
    kidney bean and okra stew with cornmeal patties 112, *113*
    spicy beef and fenugreek stew with potatoes 132, *133*

spicy beef stew with barley dough *138*, 139
spicy chickpea flour stew *114*, 115
spicy fish and onion stew 187
spicy lamb stew *150*, 151
spicy pumpkin stew 94, *95*
spicy tomato stew *70*, 71
sweet potato 83
    creamy chicken and sweet potatoes with stuffed green chilies 184

tagliatelle, teff tagliatelle with sprouted fenugreek and carrots 122, *123*
teff 16–17, 30, 98
    moringa teff lasagne 120, *121*
    one-day *injera* 24
    pasta dough 120, 122
    teff flatbread 6
    teff tagliatelle with sprouted fenugreek and carrots 122, *123*
    traditional *injera* 20–1
    whole-grain teff salad 86, *87*
tej (fermented honey wine) 10, 45, 126, 139, 156–7, 172–3
    chicken in *tej* sauce with oranges 174, *175*
telba fitfit 66
tihelo 138, 139
timatim kurt 90, *91*
tomato 34, 63, 66, 86, 89, 97, 98, 112, 132, 178, 189
    lamb-stuffed vegetables 166
    spicy tomato stew *70*, 71
    tomato salad 90, *91*
tongue
    beef tripe and tongue 143
    cabbage rolls with lamb tongue 154, *155*
tools 10–11
tosegn 39
tripe, beef tripe and tongue 143
tuiles, lacy Ethiopian tuiles with toasted barley 218, *219*
turmeric 39, 68, 89, 102, 165, 177–8, 190
    chicken simmered in a mild onion and turmeric sauce *176*, 177
    goat in mild turmeric stew with carrots 153
    potatoes and cabbage in ginger turmeric sauce 79
    potatoes and carrots in an onion turmeric sauce 88
    tender lamb cubes simmered in mild turmeric and onion sauce 152

vegetables
    buttermilk-marinated chicken with grilled vegetables 178, *179*
    lamb-stuffed vegetables 166, *167*
    vegetable salad 83
    see also specific vegetables
vinaigrette 86, 98

water, smoked milk or water 160, *161*
whole-grain bread baked in banana leaves 28, *29*

ye habesha enqulal firfir 185
yellow split pea(s) in a mild ginger and onion sauce 102
yenate telba kurs 72, *73*
yogurt, barley porridge with *niter kebbeh* and served with yogurt 58

zebu 140, 141
zilzil tibs 130
zucchini 166, 178

Acknowledgments

I would like to express my gratitude to everyone who has encouraged me through the process of writing this book. To everyone who has provided guidance, comments, network and in-kind support.

I would like to thank my mother Senait, who took the time to share all her knowledge, assisted me in reproducing several recipes, and encouraged me through all the ups and downs of this journey. To the rest of my family, especially my dad, Gebreyesus, who guided me as a writer and advised me on the Guragué culture; and my sweet sister Mardet, who is always there when I need her.

To the CY team and especially Kidist, who backed me during location shoots by handling logistics. And a special thanks to my producer, Zelalem, who offered comments, writing, and remarks.

A very warm thank you to all women all over Ethiopia; to the mothers, sisters, and daughters who have welcomed me into their homes and showed me their most precious legacy recipes.

Thanks to Chris and Kyle—without you this book would never have found its way to the global platform. Special thank you, also, to Peter for going the extra mile and taking all those beautiful pictures in the different regions of my home.

Last and certainly not least, to my friends and colleagues Hawas, Dr Kalab, Wz Konjit, Wz. Tedenekialesh, Hailu, Meherem, Assad, Wondwossen, Tesgaye, Ahmed, Anisa, and Linda who helped in many ways. To my sponsors Tomoca and Ethiopian Airlines, and to everyone in my community who constantly support the *Chef Yohanis Culinary & Lifestyle TV show,* without whom this book wouldn't be conceivable.